If I'm So Smart...
Where Did All My Money Go?

If I'm So Smart... Where Did All My Money Go?

Balancing Your Financial Objectives for Lasting Wealth

Doug Warshauer

CFMB
BOOKS

If I'm So Smart…Where Did All My Money Go?

Copyright © 2010 by Doug Warshauer.

Published in the United States by CFMB Books. Printed in the United States of America.

This publication provides general information regarding money, savings, and investments. While they information is intended to be accurate at the time of publication, investment markets, government regulations, tax laws, and other conditions are constantly changing. It is sold with the understanding that the author and publisher are not engaged in rendering financial, accounting, or other professional advice. Readers should use their own judgment and/or consult a financial expert for specific applications to their individual situation. The strategies discussed in this book are not guaranteed or warranted to produce any particular results. Both the author and the publisher specifically disclaim any responsibility for any liability, loss, or risk, personal or otherwise, which is incurred as a consequence, directly or indirectly, of the use and application of any of the contents of this book. Names and characters and situations in this book are the product of the author's imagination. Any resemblance to actual persons, living or dead, is entirely coincidental.

Cover design by Erik Hollander. HollanderDesignLab.com.
Edited by Debra Englander.
Layout and composition by Rosamond Grupp.

ISBN: 978-0-984-49374-6

Library of Congress Control Number: 2010905987

First Edition

*To my children, who hope their father
can follow his own advice*

Contents

Acknowledgements   *ix*

Introduction   *xi*

Prologue   *xix*

Big Step One – Control Spending and Debt   1

Big Step Two – Save for Short-Term Goals   37

Big Step Three – Invest Wisely   77

Big Step Four – Save for College   135

Big Step Five – Save for Retirement   195

The 18 Little Steps   *274*

Appendices   *276*

Acknowledgements

In my years of managing businesses, I have learned one thing - you can accomplish nothing alone. Writing a book is no different. Creating a book is a team effort, and I am blessed with an incredible team. If every team has a captain, the captain of my team is Lissy Peace, who is without question the greatest book publicist who has ever lived. Ever. Without her you would not be reading this right now.

Thanks also to the other key members of the team: my editor Debra Englander, whose tremendous insights and extraordinary feel for language have noticeably improved the quality of the writing; Erik Hollander, whose incredible cover design has so perfectly captured the essence of this book; and Rosamond Grupp, whose beautiful layout makes the charts and tables read naturally and helps make the book as easy to follow as I had imagined it.

While this book is about balancing your money, we all have an even more precious resource we need to balance: our time. The time I spent writing this book was time not spent elsewhere. I must offer thanks and apologies to Art Kessler, my partner at Kessler Warshauer Ventures, our private equity investment firm, who has shouldered more than his share of the load while I wrote this book; my four children, who had far too little time to play with their daddy while he was in his office writing away; and my wife Sue, who knows that I can write 300 pages about finance easier than one sentence about love, and loves me in spite of it.

Introduction

Why This Book is Important

This book has a single purpose: to help you make better financial decisions. Many people mistakenly believe that financial success depends mostly on how much they earn. Earnings are a starting point, but different people who earn the same amount can lead very different lives. You must consciously save to achieve your financial goals, and you must invest your savings wisely. Inadequate savings and poor investment often undermines financial success, even if you have sizeable earnings.

Financial decisions matter. They impact the food you eat, the clothes you wear, the car you drive, the home you own, and the neighborhood you live in. Over the long term, they determine the college your children attend and both the duration and comfort level of your retirement. Beyond material well-being, financial stress can ruin lives. If you worry about paying your credit card debt or your auto loan, or if you worry about staying current with your mortgage, undoubtedly the stress impacts your marriage and your family.

I titled this book *If I'm So Smart, Where Did All My Money Go?* to highlight the point that smart people often make bad financial decisions. If you are in financial distress or feel financially pressured, you may blame yourself, feeling your troubles must result from a personal flaw. You may feel foolish for running up debt or for investing poorly. You may feel guilty for overspending and blame yourself for a lack of self-control. The truth is that you are not foolish, nor are you over-indulgent – you simply face substantial conflicting financial demands that you have not learned to balance.

This book will teach you to balance those demands so that you can avoid financial stress and achieve lasting wealth. If you are like most Americans, on top of paying for all of life's daily expenses, you must save money for cars, homes, your children's college education, and your retirement. Your financial struggles stem from the difficulty of balancing these conflicting demands – not from any mental or moral weakness in you.

To balance these conflicting demands, you must create a financial plan that addresses each of them over your lifetime. Until now, no book has provided a personalizable program capable of helping you create that plan. This one does. It provides you very specific and *individualized* advice. For example, you will learn – based upon your own personal characteristics – how to determine precisely at what age you must start saving for retirement and what percentage of your income you must save. You will learn what objectives to save for first and which can wait until later in your life. You will also learn exactly how to invest your money for each different financial goal.

Armed with the knowledge of how much you must save to achieve each of your financial goals and how to invest your savings, your financial stress will dissipate. Your confidence in your plan will increase your ability to steadfastly follow it. This is critical – even a sound financial plan will flounder if you abandon it at the first sign of trouble. After reading this book, you will be able to set a course for yourself and stay on it. By staying on it, you will not only reach your goals, you will alleviate the stress you have about not reaching them.

Is This Fiction or Nonfiction?

Take heart, you are now reading the only dry section of this book. Beginning with the Prologue, the rest of this book is fiction. It is a story, complete with a protagonist, a collection of colorful minor characters, and, of course, a wise teacher. Most of the characters are smart people who somehow seem to make poor financial decisions. Admittedly, the plot is modest, just enough to keep the story going. The usual disclaimer about none of the characters representing any real person applies.

People learn and remember more effectively thorough story-telling. Since my mission is to teach you how to make better financial decisions, my success depends upon your internalizing the lessons presented. A logical argument, no matter how persuasive, is easily forgotten. By wrapping the argument within the framework of a story, by embodying the concepts within characters, I hope to assist you in learning how to apply the principles of effective money management to you're your own individual situation.

The story consists primarily of a hypothetical financial planning seminar. This narrative device allows for the interaction of a variety of people with different ages, incomes, and preferences. Hopefully, most of you will see something of yourselves in one or more of the characters. The more you can relate the ideas to your own life as you are reading, the more effectively you will be able to apply them when you create your own financial plan.

What You Will Learn

To better manage your money, you need a complete lifetime financial plan. For example, you cannot save for your retirement without first saving for your children's college education. The college bills come due sooner, and you could find yourself eating into your retirement funds to pay for college. Similarly, you cannot save to buy a house if you do not budget your annual expenses adequately. If you spend too much, you will accumulate either too little savings for a down payment or too much credit card debt to qualify for a sufficient mortgage. Your financial plan must cover all aspects of your financial life.

Because the idea of a lifetime financial plan might seem daunting, I have divided the process into steps. There are only five big steps: controlling spending and debt, saving for short-term goals, investing wisely, saving for college, and saving for retirement. Each big step consists of three or four little steps. By the end of the book, you will have a step-by-step guide to creating your own lifetime financial plan.

For many people, the financial plan begins with debt reduction. If you have accumulated consumer or credit card debt, your plan must set a course toward eliminating that debt by budgeting your annual expenditures at sustainable levels. If you have already tried cutting your expenses and found it hard to find the needed savings, this book will help. Rather than general advice such as "write down everything you spend, and determine what you can eliminate," you will find specific guidance about what percentage of your income you should be spending on housing, transportation, food, and every other category. This information will help you determine where you are spending too much, and where you should look to find your savings.

The financial plan must also cover the two most expensive items most people buy: homes and cars. This book will help you answer key housing related questions such as: "When should I buy my first house?" "How long should I stay in my house before moving?" "How much can I afford to pay for a house?" and "How should I finance my home purchase?" It will also address key auto related questions such as "How much can I afford to spend on a car?" "How long should I keep my car?" and "Should I buy or lease?" Effectively managing the purchases of your major assets will enable you to live in the most comfortable homes and drive the most desirable cars your income can support. It also will prevent you from making mistakes in home or car buying which put you in debt or impair your long term goals such as college and retirement saving.

If you have children, college savings may be a major part of your financial plan. You know college is expensive. You probably know that the cost of college has risen faster than overall inflation. But if you are like most people, your knowledge ends there. What will college cost when your children are ready? Will you be able to get financial aid, and if so, how much? Will your child choose an expensive private school or a less expensive state school? What will you be earning then and how much will you be able to afford to pay? The overwhelming uncertainty forces most people to throw up their hands and think, "I'll save what I can and hope for the best. What else can I do?" The truth is, you can do a lot. Most of those questions are not as difficult as they seem. Using the information in this book, you will be able to develop a college savings plan that you know will be sufficient to pay for your children's college education.

Finally, retirement. Like saving for college, saving for retirement entails tremendous uncertainty -- how much you will earn over the course of your life, how much your savings will grow, what real purchasing power your dollars will have when you are retired, how old you will be when you retire, how long you and your spouse will live, and what, if any, social security you will receive. Once again, the questions may seem unanswerable, but they are not. You will learn how to accurately estimate the answers to those questions, and in doing so to formulate a retirement plan that will give you the confidence that you *will* be able to retire, and that you *will* be able to live comfortably in retirement. You will learn just how much of your income you must save to achieve your retirement goals, and at what age you must begin saving for retirement.

Saving for everything in your plan, including auto, home, college, and retirement, requires effective investment of your saved dollars. If you are saving to buy a house, and you invest your money in stocks, a drop in the value of those stocks can force you to buy a less desirable house or defer your home purchase for years. If you are saving for retirement, and the cost of living grows by more than your investments, you may find yourself unable to afford to maintain your lifestyle. A faulty investment plan can undermine an excellent savings plan. This book will show you how to choose an appropriate investment strategy for each of your various financial goals.

How These Recommendations Were Derived

I come to financial planning via a different route than most authors of personal finance books. Many writers of these books are career financial planners, well-schooled in the standard strategies and techniques of financial planning. These books offer extensive detail on various laws, rules, and regulations. Unfortunately, their advice is often too general to help you create a lifelong financial plan that works for you.

Successful stock market investors comprise the other major category of writers of personal finance books. Their books allow the general public a glimpse of the investment secrets that made them millions. I feel a little less charitable toward most of these books. (You'll see why when you come to the investment recommendations here.)

I have spent most of my career investing in and managing private businesses. The long term business forecast is the primary tool of my trade. To predict how much money a business will earn over its lifetime, you must build a financial model which accounts for each of the factors that will influence the business' performance. The models can then demonstrate the impact of changes in any of the variables, such as the rate of sales growth or the interest rate. Over the years, I have developed considerable expertise in constructing such models.

The recognition that families' financial lives can be similarly modeled represents the critical insight in the development of this book, and the recommendations in it spring from the inescapable conclusions of the financial models. Using modeling techniques, I can answer such questions as "How much sooner can I retire if I save 6% of my income instead of 8%?" or "How much sooner can I buy a house if my stock investments go up 10% per year instead of 6% per year?"

The calculations that support the recommendations have been made on a simple spreadsheet. To the extent possible, those calculations have been presented, either in the *Let's Do the Math* sections within the text, or in the Appendices. I recognize that many people fear math. That fear, in part, exacerbates the uncertainty in financial planning. As much as possible, I have tried to take the mystery out of the calculations, so that you can understand and have confidence in the thought process behind the recommendations.

All the information that underlies the calculations is publicly available, either in books or on the internet. Although some of the calculations are complex, none use abstract statistical techniques. All of the recommendations and conclusions follow simple logic and common sense. Achieving lasting wealth does not require extraordinary intelligence – it simply requires a sound financial plan. I hope that by presenting the facts in a direct and engaging way, you will find it possible to create an effective plan for yourself.

One More Time: Why This Book is So Important

The financial decisions you make today have an impact on the rest of your life. Poor financial decisions have a domino effect. Fall into debt today, and future interest payments will compound tomorrow's challenges. The extra income you would have been able sock away as retirement savings will instead go to your creditors. Retirement will recede further into the future as you attempt to recover from the mistakes of the past.

Good financial decisions occur when people have a plan they believe in. Without confidence in their plan, people make decisions haphazardly, abandoning prior decisions as the market swings. By offering advice specific to your personal circumstances, this book will help you create a plan you can stick to. You will know how much you need to save to achieve your individual goals. You will believe in your investment strategy, so you won't second-guess yourself each time the market takes a sharp move up or down.

It will not take long for you to see the results. If you are currently in debt, you will be able to develop a plan which quickly reduces your debt. Soon, you will be free of debt and able to put away real savings. If you are trying to save for your children's college education or for your retirement, you will see your savings build steadily, and you will know, regardless of the fluctuations of the stock market, that you are maximizing your chances of achieving your goals.

Building confidence has another benefit, perhaps even more important than the actual achievement of your goals. You will see your financial stress melt away. Knowing that you are on the right path matters. By eliminating the nagging worry that you have made bad decisions, you free yourself to accept whatever outcome you encounter. Understanding the range of possible outcomes, and having a back-up plan for all of them, allows you to face the future without fear.

The confidence and security that you feel will spill over into all aspects of your life. When you are worried about your finances, you cannot fully enjoy anything you purchase, because you feel guilty that you overspent. Once you believe in your financial plan, you will be amazed by how much more freely you can enjoy that luxury vacation, fancy dinner, or expensive new outfit. Even better, marital conflict over money may dissipate, allowing you and your spouse to enjoy a healthier and less stressful relationship. These are but a few examples of the many benefits of financial confidence. And they are yours for the taking.

Prologue

Joe's Story

Not long ago, in his spacious apartment in a fashionable district of a large American city, a forlorn young man sat at his desk staring at his credit card bills. He added the amount due on each card and frowned at the total: just shy of $20,000. He added them again to be sure, but he had calculated correctly; he was $20,000 in debt. "Not possible," he thought. How could he have so much debt when he was making so much money?

Thinking back over the past year, Joe replayed in his mind the series of events that led him to his present predicament. Less than twelve months ago he had graduated from college with good if not outstanding grades, solidly in the top third of his class. The economy was still strong then, and with his double major in business and accounting he'd had a variety of job offers. When he selected the job in banking, at a first year salary of $48,000, he imagined he had struck it rich at the age of twenty-two.

Where did all that money go? He had no obvious answer. He had taken a vacation in Mexico a few months ago, one last "spring break" with his friends who were still in college. But that trip couldn't have cost more than $2,000, probably less. Other than that, he hadn't splurged on anything. His apartment, while impressive, was hardly different than those rented by the thousands of other young single professionals in the area. He'd leased a new Honda

SUV, back before gas prices skyrocketed. But again, how was that different than the millions of Americans also driving around in SUVs?

Joe felt disappointed in himself. He considered himself financially sophisticated. As a banker, he spent his days evaluating whether businesses had enough income to pay their debts. One would think he'd have enough sense to stay out of debt himself. The more he brooded, the more distressed he became. "How much damage had he done to his future?" he worried. "When would he be able to buy the condo he'd been eyeing? Will his children, assuming he has children eventually, be able to go to college? Will he be able to retire?

By the next morning, his fear had morphed into a determination to solve his problems. Immediately after work, he drove to a local bookstore and purchased a number of books on personal finance. Joe read every spare moment for the next few weeks.

Most of the books he read emphasized thrift. No doubt, he had been spending too much. He knew he needed to curtail his spending, but, even after reading all those books, he was not sure how. What was he spending too much on? And exactly how much less did he need to spend? He needed more specific answers.

Returning to the bookstore to continue his search, Joe bumped into an older colleague. "Any recommendations?" Joe asked as they browsed the Personal Finance stocks.

"Yes, but a seminar, not a book," the colleague replied. "A few years ago I went to a seminar unlike anything I'd read or heard before. It changed my life. The seminar was called "Balancing Your Financial Objectives for Lasting Wealth."

"What was so different about it?" Joe asked.

"Specifics," said the colleague, "the seminar helps you develop specific answers to help you achieve your own financial goals."

"I could use some specifics," Joe replied, "I am worried that I've screwed up all my future goals already."

His colleague was comforting. "Don't worry. This seminar will help you think about the long term. It's really unique."

Two weeks later, Joe was driving his Honda SUV to the seminar's first session.

Control Spending and Debt

CHAPTER 1

Income and Expenses

J oe poked his head into the seminar room a few minutes before its scheduled start time. Judging from the absence of sound emerging from the room, he had expected to find few, if any, participants inside. Instead, he observed at least a dozen people, silently sipping coffee and maintaining an uncomfortable distance from each other. He felt somewhat surprised to discover that he was easily the youngest of the participants. Despite having learned of the seminar from a colleague at least twenty years his senior, and having read the brochure description which advertised the seminar to people of all ages, Joe nevertheless carried with him the subconscious expectations of one who has spent most of his life in age-segregated schools. Instinctively, he wandered toward a youngish couple who, though likely around thirty years old, seemed closest of anyone to Joe's generation.

The woman interrupted her conversation as Joe approached. Smiling warmly, she introduced herself. "Hi, I'm Sally, and this is my husband Eric." The three shook hands. After a few moments of friendly chit-chat, the conversation turned toward the subject of the seminar. Sally was not one to beat around the bush.

"You don't have children yet, do you?" she asked Joe.

"No, not even a girlfriend right now."

"We have two kids. Our son is four, and our daughter just turned one. You're smart to be here now. I wish we had come to one of these before we had children."

"Why?" Joe asked.

"Once you have children, finances get so complicated. We bought a house five years ago, before our son was born," Sally began and then stopped, noticing Eric's perturbed expression. She turned to him. "What? We are going to be talking about money in front of everyone for the next five weeks." She turned back to Joe.

"When we bought the house, the housing market was booming. We figured we'd stay a few years, until we had another baby. It's not ideal for two kids. But by the time our daughter was born, the house probably lost 20% of its value. I don't think we could sell it for enough to cover our mortgage."

"We can pay the mortgage," Eric interrupted, "it's not like we can't just stay there and wait for the value to bounce back."

Sally leaned perceptibly closer to Joe. "It's really too small." She spoke in a quiet, almost conspiratorial tone.

Eric responded, "Moving to a bigger house would mean a bigger mortgage, which would be fine if we didn't have to start saving for college. Do you know what it will cost to send two children to college in twenty years?" Eric, though directing his eyes at Joe, seemed focused on his wife. The conversation was beginning to make Joe uncomfortable. This couple, who at first seemed warm and friendly, appeared to have their own tensions. At that moment, Joe's discomfort was relieved by the announcement, "Please everyone, take your seats." The instructor, unbeknownst to Joe, Eric, and Sally, had just entered the room. The seats, small wooden cushionless folding chairs, were arranged in a circle to facilitate discussion. The mild discomfort of the chairs appeared to reflect and perhaps enhance the unease of the participants seated in them.

The instructor sat down in the circle, too. To the right of his seat, instead of another chair, stood a small easel with a blank, white flip-chart on it. "Welcome to Balancing Your Financial Objectives for Lasting Wealth," he began, once all the participants were in their seats. "We will spend the next five weeks together discussing our financial problems, something most people consider private. We are not used to sharing financial details with others, especially not in large groups.

"This is not group therapy. You will not solve your financial problems just by talking about them. But you need to be comfortable talking about your financial problems in front of this group so that we can help you deal with them."

"Are you going to call on us?" asked one participant. The group chuckled nervously.

"Yes. No one will be put on the spot, but I am going to rely on all of you to participate, ask questions, and join in the discussion," the instructor answered. "Okay, let's get to work. Today's session will focus on budgeting your expenditures and on debt. Raise your hand if you have any debt. Credit card debt, consumer debt, a mortgage, a home equity loan, an auto loan, a student loan, any debt at all."

Slowly, the hands went up. Everyone raised a hand.

"That's not a surprise," said the instructor. "Frankly, if anyone had not raised a hand, I would have been surprised. Not just because this is a personal finance seminar, but because this is America. In America, almost everyone has some kind of debt."

He pointed at Joe. "Tell us your name, a little about you and your family, and tell us what kind of debt you have?"

"My name is Joe. I'm 23 years old. I work in banking. I have a lot of credit card debt."

"How much?"

"Twenty thousand dollars."

"That is a lot. Do you have a mortgage, too?"

"No." Though he had been eager to buy a home, Joe felt somehow relieved he'd been able to answer that question negatively.

"How about you?" asked the instructor, pointing to a woman sitting a few seats down from Joe.

"I'm Andrea," she says, "I'm a single mother of a ten year old girl. I have a lot of debt. I do have a mortgage and I also have a lot of credit card debt. I know I shouldn't, but I can't help it. After paying the mortgage and all the bills, there's just nothing left. I make sure to put something away for college, because I've always heard you pay yourself first, but each month the credit card balance gets higher. And I know I'm not supposed to do that because the interest on the credit cards is ridiculous. I guess that's why I'm here."

This time, the instructor didn't need to call on anyone. Sally jumped right in, "I know what you mean. We have two kids," she waved her thumb back and forth between her and Eric, "and we are trying to save as much as we can for college. We also max out our 401k plans, because we know you're supposed to save as much as you can when you're young. But we both work, so we need to pay for day care and preschool. Add that to paying our mortgage and all the other expenses and it's just impossible. I mean, between the two of us we make a lot of money, and we still can't seem to pay off our credit cards."

Eric had appeared to concur until the comment about making a lot of money. "I'm not sure we make *a lot* of money," he corrected. "We sure don't seem to make enough to buy everything we want."

Most of the group nodded sympathetically to that statement. The instructor jumped back into the conversation. "Few people can buy everything they want. Part of the solution to your debt problem will be figuring out exactly what you can and cannot afford. Once you learn how to set your spending at a level that is appropriate for your income, you will be well on your way to eliminating your debt once and for all."

He paused allowing that message to reverberate through the classroom. "You were all asked to bring with you a summary of all your expenditures for the past year. Take them out now, we're going to go over them."

Joe removed the budget he had prepared from a shiny leather briefcase. As instructed by the preparation materials he'd received a few weeks earlier, Joe had dug through the past twelve months of cancelled checks and credit card statements like a paleontologist recovering dispersed dinosaur fossils. He had reassembled his expenses, as closely as possible, into a shape resembling their true form. Or, rather, he reassembled them into a format specified in the seminar instructions, with each individual expense grouped into predefined categories. When complete, his expenditure summary, labeled Worksheet #1, looked as follows:

Worksheet #1
Annual Household Expenditures

Housing	$13,800
Transportation	$ 8,800
Food	$ 9,000
Entertainment	$ 5,300
Household furnishings	$ 5,000
Clothing	$ 1,800
Household/personal consumables	$ 600
Medical expenses	$ 0
Miscellaneous	$ 600
Total Household Expenditures	**$44,900**

"Let's begin at the bottom," starts the instructor. "You have all estimated on one sheet of paper your annual expenditures for the past year. You were asked to allocate those expenditures into certain categories. I'll explain why in a minute. First, though, look at the total. This is how much you spent. Now, on another page, you were asked to calculate your total family net income. Take out that page, too."

Joe again reached into his briefcase and pulled out another page he'd prepared, labeled Worksheet #2. It looked as follows:

Worksheet #2	
Annual Household Net Income	
Gross Employment Income	$48,000
FICA tax (SS + Medicare)	$ 3,672
Employee Med Insurance Contribution	$ 2,400
Federal Income Tax	$ 5,389
State Income Tax	$ 1,796
Net Income	**$34,742**

When everyone seemed ready, the instructor continued. "Let's make sure you have done this correctly. To calculate your total family net income, you start with your total family gross income, then subtract FICA tax, which includes Social Security and Medicare, federal income taxes, state income taxes, and the payroll deduction that represents your contribution for health insurance. What's left is your net income. You can find all these numbers on your paycheck every two weeks and on your W-2 at the end of the year."

"Can't we just take these numbers from our tax return?" interrupted one of the participants.

"No," answered the instructor, "for most people it is better to use your W-2 for gross income, FICA tax, and health care contributions. You tax return includes investment income, and it also includes various allowances and deductions. Right now, we only want to know how much you earned from work."

"Do you want us to use the numbers from our W-2 for federal and state income tax? I thought we were supposed to use our tax return for those," said Andrea.

The instructor smiled broadly. "Excellent question Andrea. The numbers on your W-2 for federal and state income taxes tell you the amount your company withheld from your paycheck. But those are not your actual tax liability. You need to use your tax return for your actual tax liability."

Another participant, Mark, raised his hand. "What about payroll deductions for 401(k) contributions? Should we also deduct those now?"

The instructor shook his head. "No, we don't want to subtract those yet. First we want to calculate how much net income we have and what our expenses are before we decide how much, if anything, we'll contribute to a 401(k)."

Mark looked dissatisfied. "I always put the maximum into my 401(k). I pay way too much in taxes already and don't plan to give the government any more of my money than I have to. The way I see it, this should come out first, so I don't pretend I have money to spend that is really not there."

Judging from the nodding of heads around the room, Mark had struck a nerve. Joe joined the chorus, "Are you saying that we should not contribute to our 401(k)? I know we're all here for help, but if there is one thing you hear over and over, it's that you need to contribute to your 401(k)."

"Don't worry," replied the instructor, "we won't ignore the 401(k). But we won't take it as a given, either. Sometimes you want to contribute to your 401(k), and sometimes you don't. Plus, when you do contribute, you need to learn to determine how much. We will get to all of that in a few weeks. Right now, all we want to do is compare how much you are earning and how much you are spending. We call the amount you earn your "Net Income." That is the amount at the bottom of Worksheet #2. The amount you are spending is at the bottom of the Worksheet #1."

At this point, the instructor turned to the flip chart standing next to his chair. With a black marker, in big block letters, he wrote:

> **STEP #1: IF YOU ARE SPENDING**
>
> **MORE THAN YOU ARE EARNING,**
>
> **YOU MUST EITHER START EARNING**
>
> **MORE OR SPENDING LESS.**

Mark, still dissatisfied after the 401(k) conversation, looked even more peeved now. "Isn't that a bit obvious? I'm sure none of us came to this seminar to learn that."

The instructor, not oblivious to the aggressive tone of Mark's voice, frowned. "Do you all think this is obvious? Let's see if everyone agrees. Raise your hand if feel that you knew this already."

People looked left and right. First, one hand rose, then another, and another, until finally everyone had a hand up. A number of people shifted uncomfortably. Their facial expressions reflected the concern that this seminar would fail them, as they had failed in all their prior attempts to improve their financial footing. The participants' glances darted from person to person, avoiding eye contact with the instructor.

"Okay," the instructor started again. He was still frowning, or at least he was trying to, but a whisper of a smile snuck through. "Since apparently no one has learned anything here yet, let me ask another question. Look at the two pages you have in front of you. How many of you have a bigger number on the net income page than the expenditure page?"

The tone of the class turned at this moment. Only two people kept their hands raised. The others, who a moment earlier had been eyeing each other in tacit revolution, lowered their gazes toward their laps. The instructor drove the point home. "Unfortunately, it is not always easy to achieve the obvious. Of course you don't need me to tell you that you must spend less than you earn. *You need me to help you balance the conflicting objectives that lead you to spend more than your earn.* Beginning with getting out of debt, this seminar will concentrate on explaining some seemingly obvious concepts, and it will provide you the tools to manage your money so that you are able do what you intuitively know you should."

CHAPTER TWO

The Expenditure Budget

A fter a brief break, the attendees resettled into their seats. The next portion of the seminar would cover their expenditures in detail. Joe felt ready. The dramatic conclusion to the first part of the seminar gave him confidence that real answers would be forthcoming. Comparing his net income to his expenditures, he could not avoid the conspicuous fact that he'd spent $10,000 more than his net income. That accounted for the credit card bills. But he still could not envision how he would reduce his spending so dramatically.

The instructor's voice interrupted Joe's thoughts. "We'll discuss each expense category one by one, starting with housing. For nearly everyone, housing costs more than anything else. Use the pocket calculators you were asked to bring. Divide the total amount you spent on housing by your net income. That calculation will tell you the percent of your net income you spent on housing. Remember, your housing expense includes everything related to housing. If you own your home, you must include your mortgage, real estate taxes, association dues, repairs and maintenance, and utilities. If you are a renter you probably only have rent and utilities. Understand? When you finish your calculation, just shout out your numbers."

"Forty-two percent."

"Thirty-nine."

"Twenty-eight percent."

The numbers ranged from the high twenties to close to fifty percent. "If you are below 35%," started the instructor, "I have good and bad news. The good news is that you are not overspending on housing. The bad news is that, if you need to cut your expenses, you may have to cut elsewhere. For those of you over 35%, and it seemed like more than half the group, as a rule you are spending too much of your net income on housing. By reducing your housing expenses to a more normal level, given your income, you can bring your expenses in line with your income."

The hands shot up. Eric did not wait to be called on. "Doesn't that percentage depend on the city you live in? I mean, housing costs a fortune here. If we lived in a more rural area, or in another state, wouldn't we automatically spend less on housing?"

Another man agreed. "There's no way I can spend only 35% of my net income on housing. No chance at all. Not if I want my family to live in a safe neighborhood."

"I couldn't cut down to 35% if I wanted to," added another, "My mortgage is what it is. I can't get it lower, and I can't sell my house. Not in this housing market. So I'm at 40% and staying there."

The instructor held up his hand to stop the mutiny. This was a passionate group, no doubt about it. They had real problems and needed real solutions. "Housing is the toughest expense. Because it costs so much, it offers the greatest opportunity for savings. On the other hand, it can be the least flexible, especially for people who already own their homes.

"Keep a couple of points in mind. First, housing prices do vary greatly across the United States. They vary far more than incomes. Therefore, in areas where housing is expensive, you may have to spend more than 35% of your net income on housing to live where you want to live. That just means you'll have to find extra savings in some other category.

"Second, renters have certain advantages. They can move to a less expensive home without first needing to sell their home. So if you are currently renting, you have a better chance to find opportunities to reduce your housing expense. Also, renters typically pay less to live in the same home than owners. That makes it easier for them to stay under 35%."

Mark interrupted again. "Renters may pay less, but owners build up equity in their home. Part of the mortgage payment is principal, and paying principal is like saving money."

"Very true," responded the instructor. "Still, even if you take principal payments into account, owning a home can be expensive compared to renting. We will discuss all the pros and cons of home ownership next week. We'll examine how much to spend on a house, how to finance it, when to buy and when to rent. For now, just keep in mind that 35% is your target for housing expenditures. Let's move on to transportation expenses."

The consternation on the faces of the participants showed that they weren't yet comfortable with the housing issue. Many open issues remained, and the instructor knew it. "I know you still have questions about housing. We are far from done with our housing discussion. Today's discussion is about building a budget you can afford, and for this purpose, all you need to recognize is that housing should represent about 35% of your net income. We will go through all the different expense categories today and give you a target for each one. These targets will help you analyze your own budget, and see where you are spending more than perhaps you should."

Sally, looking skeptical, raised her hand. "Where do these targets come from? Did you set them?"

"The targets come from surveys done by the Bureau of Labor Statistics, which is part of the U.S. Department of Labor. They periodically survey thousands of Americans, asking how they spend their money. We have taken that survey data and linked it to people's net income, to highlight what percent of net income people spend on each category."

Sally pounced: "So your guidelines are really averages of what Americans spend. But everyone isn't the same. I might want to spend a lot of money on my house, but someone else might be really into their car. Won't our spending patterns be different? My sister, for example, is always buying new clothes. I'm sure she spends more than the average person on clothing. How are these guidelines going to help her or any of us if they don't account for individual differences?"

There was considerable agreement on Sally's point. But another contingent saw a flaw in Sally's argument. Andrea spoke up for that group. "Sure, we all have differences. But that doesn't have to be a problem. If you spend more in one area, you just have to spend less in another, right?" She looked at the instructor, who nodded encouragingly. "I am spending 38% of my net income on housing, which I guess is 3% too high. But as long as I am spending 3% below the target somewhere else, I think I'll be okay."

"Is that right?" one participant asked, looking at the instructor.

The instructor nodded. "It's exactly right. You will know the target amounts for each spending category. All together, they add up to 90% of net income. If you spend at the target level in each category, you will save 10% of your net income each year. If you exceed the target in one category but compensate by spending below the target in another, you will still save 10% of your net income. On the other hand, if you exceed the target in many or most categories, you will spend beyond your means.

"The category targets allow you to compare your spending patterns to average Americans. Most people find this knowledge very empowering. Suppose you discover that you are spending 39% of your net income on housing, which is 4% over the target. You now can make an informed decision. You are spending a higher percentage of your income on housing than do most Americans. Is that consistent with your personal preferences? Do you live in an area that requires overemphasizing housing? If not, you will want to reduce your housing expenses. If you need to maintain your current housing expenses, you know that you need to spend below average in some other area."

The instructor paused, to give everyone time to reflect on his comments and to wait for any further objections. No hands went up. "Any more questions before we go back to transportation?"

Still no hands. That bridge crossed, the instructor started again. "Okay, calculate the percent of your net income you spent on transportation. This includes any car lease payment, loan payment or down payment. It also includes gas, repairs and maintenance, auto insurance, parking fees and other auto related expenses. Plus, it includes the cost of public transportation." He waited while people made their calculations. "Everyone ready? The target for transportation expenses is 15% of net income."

Once again, a few hands immediately rose. Joe spoke first. "Won't this calculation be skewed if you bought a car this year? Mine is coming out to over 30%, but that's partly because I made a down payment on a new car I leased this year."

"Yes," answered the instructor, "we need to account for that. How much was your down payment?"

"$3,000."

"And how long is your lease?"

"Three years."

"Divide the down payment by the number of years of your lease. If you had bought the car instead of leased it, you would divide by the number of years you expect to own the car. With a $3,000 down payment and a three year lease, you should only count $1,000 in the calculation of your transportation costs."

The instructor surveyed the group. "If you have the same issue as Joe, go ahead and re-calculate your transportation costs. By the same token, if you made a down payment in prior years for a car you are still driving, try to estimate how much of that down payment should be allocated to your transportation costs this year."

"What do you mean?" asked Andrea.

"Suppose Joe made that same $3,000 down payment on his car, but instead of leasing it this year he leased it 1 ½ years ago. If he doesn't include some amount of that down payment in calculating his transportation costs, he will understate them. Regardless of when he acquired the car, he should have $1,000 of "down payment" expense as part of his total transportation expenditure."

"I think I get it," said Andrea, "you try to count the average down payment expense, so the transportation expense doesn't change in years when you buy a car."

"Exactly. Now everyone, go ahead and recalculate your total transportation expense."

After a few moments, the group looked ready. Joe looked at his own worksheet. In addition to the $1,000 he counted from the down payment, he also had spent $400 per month, or $4,800, on his lease payments, so the cost of the car alone was $5,800. It was brand new and under warranty, so he'd spent nothing on repairs and maintenance. That was good. But he'd spent about $1,800 on gas (because of lousy mileage) and $1,200 on insurance. The total was $8,800. This was a full 25% of his net income of just under $35,000!

Worksheet 2-1
Joe's Transportation Expenses

Down Payment	$1,000
($3,000 down payment ÷ 3 years)	
Lease Payments	$4,800
Repairs & Maintenance	$ 0
Gas	$1,800
Insurance	$1,200
Total Expenses	**$8,800**
Net Income	$34,742
Percent of Net Income Spent on Transportation	**25%**
(8,000÷34,742)	

"Those of you who are spending more than 15% of net income on transportation are spending above the target," said the instructor. "Raise your hand if you are in that group." As with housing, most people raised their hands. "It is normal that most of you are over-spending on transportation, just as it is normal that you are overspending on housing. When people get into trouble and spend more than they can afford, they nearly always overspend in either housing or transportation, if not both. These are the two biggest categories, and they offer the most opportunities for spending too much. That's why we will spend nearly all of next week discussing housing and auto purchases in great detail."

"What do we do if we are over in both housing and auto?" asked one woman. "I understood that if we were spending too much on housing, we could make it up somewhere else. But if we are spending too much on housing and auto, will we be able to make up both of them somewhere else?"

"Probably not," answered the instructor. "You need to find savings in at least one of those categories. When we discuss the other categories, you'll see that they provide fewer savings opportunities. Transportation offers lots of savings opportunities." He scans the group. "Does anyone have suggestions on how to save your transportation dollars?"

"Sell the car!" shouted one man. Everyone laughed. "I'm at least half serious," he continued. "I'm looking at my number, and I'm at 23%. I could get way below 15% if I eliminate my car payments, my insurance payments, my parking fees, and my gas bills. I take the train to work twice a week as it is. If I took the train the other three days and we used my wife's car the rest of the time, I could get rid of all that. And I'd probably even make a couple thousand selling the car."

"That's lucky for you," answered another man. "I'd be under-water on my loan if I tried to sell my car. Plus, there's no way I could get by without a car. I think I'm stuck. I don't see how I can realistically lower my transportation expenses, even if they are 18% of my net income."

"I'm underwater, too," added another. "Does it ever make sense to sell your car, even if the sales proceeds are less than your auto loan?"

"Sometimes it does," said the instructor. "It depends how much you can save by changing cars and how "underwater" you are on the loan. By trading down to a less expensive car, the savings in your car payments and insurance payments could catch up to the initial loss you must take when selling your current car. The more expensive your current car is, the better your chances of that working for you."

Joe thought about the 25% of net income he spent on transportation. No doubt the Honda SUV was a mistake. He hoped he could exchange it for a cheaper car, even though he had two years left on his lease. Reducing his housing expense would be easier because his apartment lease was up soon.

"Now that we have covered the two major expenses," said the instructor, "we'll proceed more quickly through the other expenses. The good thing about these expenses is that you aren't normally locked into them. If you own a home or a car, or if you lease a car, reducing your expense can take a while, and it may be impractical. All the other expense categories consist mostly of day-to-day discretionary purchases. You can usually start spending less on them immediately.

"Unfortunately, they account for much less of your spending. You may be able to squeeze a few percent here and there, but these categories offer fewer opportunities for substantial savings."

The instructor turned to his flip chart and wrote the list of other categories: Food, Entertainment, Household Furnishings, Clothing, Household/Personal Supplies and Expenses, Medical, and Miscellaneous. He sat back down. "Let's start with food. It is by far the largest category left. The target expenditure on food is 14% of net income. How do you all compare with that?"

Andrea spoke up, "When I was totaling my expenditures at home, I couldn't believe how much I was spending on food. I am around 18% of net income, and we only have two of us. Over the last week before this meeting, I've been really trying to cut back."

"How have you cut back?"

"First, we've been eating at home more. It's easier for me to go out, since I don't usually feel like cooking when I get home from work. But eating at home is much less expensive. When we do go out, we've been trying to select less expensive restaurants. Also, I switched from shopping at one of those premium stores to one that is more of a discounter."

"I don't know if I'd want to change grocery stores," said another woman. I really like the one near me, plus I think it's better quality. But I'm sure I could choose less expensive foods just by being a bit more conscious of what everything costs. You know, more chicken and less steak."

Joe piped in, "I eat out a lot, and I'd hate to change that. But I'm sure I could start making my coffee at home, and that would save me a couple dollars a day, which adds up to nearly $1,000 a year."

"Good," said the instructor, "It's easy to find savings in the food category. There are lots of ways to do it, and you can begin changing how much you spend immediately. If you are spending more than 14% of your net income on food, you should figure out how you will bring that number down. If you cannot get your housing or transportation numbers down to their target, food may be your best opportunity to make up for excess spending. Let's move on to entertainment. The target for entertainment spending is 6% of net income. What are all of you spending on entertainment?"

"What exactly counts as entertainment?" asked a woman.

"That's a good question. Think of entertainment as anything you do or buy primarily for fun. It includes the cost of activities and services like air travel, hotels, movies, baseball games, health club dues, and piano lessons. It also includes the cost of products such as cameras, DVDs, and golf clubs."

"Well, this category should be easy to cut," said one participant. "Everything in it is completely optional."

Another man didn't seem so sure. "I guess they are optional. But it includes all the things I really like to do. I'm at 9% now, and I think I'd be miserable if I had to cut out 1/3 of these expenses to get down to 6%. I'd rather cut my housing expense to 32% and stay at 9% on my entertainment expenses."

"Not me," answered the first participant. "Anyway, I own my house and am not moving, so I'm stuck with my housing at 40%. My entertainment is 7% now, and I think I could cut it to 4 or 5% without minding a bit."

The group listened to both people. They weren't sure who was right. They turned to the instructor like the crowd at a baseball game turns to the umpire after a close play at home plate. "I like this discussion," said the instructor. "I like that you are starting to think about the trade-offs between the categories, how it is okay to go over in one category as long as you make it up somewhere else. Everyone's budget should reflect their own priorities."

He paused, giving everyone time to apply that thought to their individual situation. "Let's go on to Household Furnishings. The target for this is 5% of net income. How are you doing on this one?"

"Not well," said Joe. "I spent 14% on household furnishings. I moved into my apartment this year and had to buy all kinds of furniture."

"Isn't this kind of like an auto purchase?" asked Mark. You don't spend much most years, but every once in a while you have a large expense."

The instructor agreed. "That's very true. You could treat home furnishings like a car down payment, but it would be very complicated. You buy many different items for your house, and each lasts a different length of time. It's too unwieldy to try to allocate all those purchases. Instead, just think of the 5% target as the amount you will spend most years on household furnishings such as beds, sofas, tables, ovens, refrigerators, and televisions."

"What should you do in the years you move and spend more than the target?"

"Either cut back in other categories that year, or, better yet, if you have allocated some of the prior years' savings for this purpose, the money you need will be waiting when you move. Next session, when we discuss saving for a home, we will discuss saving enough so you can buy furniture to fill up your new home. For now, let's focus now on years that you do not move, for which 5% should be sufficient."

"This seems like an easy category to cut back on, or at least to put off," said one woman. "I was thinking of buying a new sofa, mostly because I'm tired of the old one. But it will cost a few thousand dollars, and I don't really need it now."

"Great point," said the instructor. "If you are in debt right now, the Household Furnishings category may offer you a good chance to save a few percent. Sometimes you can't put things off – if, say, your hot water heater breaks. But many times you can postpone buying these items for a couple years, until you have paid off your debt and are in a better position to buy them. The next category is clothing. The target for clothing is 5% of net income. If you haven't found your savings yet, I hope you can find them here. After this, although we have three categories to go, any savings are hard to achieve."

"Well, I'm way over on this one," exclaimed one woman. "I spend that in December alone!"

"Me, too. I don't see how I could get down to 5% of net income. I'm a little embarrassed to say it, but the clothes I wear just cost too much."

"I was right on 5%," said Joe. "I could definitely cut back next year. I had to buy some new suits when I started my job, but now that I have them I don't need more. Next year I could probably spend only 2 or 3%."

"I think you are all getting a feel for the choices before you," said the instructor. "If you are overspending in food, you can look for savings in housing, or transportation, or entertainment, or household furnishings, or clothing. This is a major component of balancing your objectives. You can build a budget that fits your lifestyle and personal preferences."

The instructor looked at his watch. The discussion had left them a few minutes behind schedule. No matter, he thought, they can get through the last three categories quickly. "The next category is Household/Personal Supplies and Expenses. These typically represent 5% of net income."

"What is that?" asked one woman.

"All the little things you buy for your home or yourself. Soaps, shampoos, and cosmetics. Cleaning supplies. Books and magazines. Paper goods like toilet paper and tissues."

"Can you save much on that stuff?"

"Most people can't. Few people overspend much in this category. It's hard to spend far below the target, too. You might be able to be a little more cost conscious about the items you choose or the store you purchase them from. But it's hard to use less soap or toilet paper. If you count on saving much from this category, you'll probably fall short."

The instructor looked ready to continue, but Andrea stopped him. "When I was categorizing my expenses last week, I found it almost impossible to separate household supplies from food. I buy them both at the same stores. When I look back at my credit card statements and my cancelled checks, I know where I shopped and how much I spent, but not what I bought there. I can't determine what I spent on food and what on household supplies."

"Did anyone else have that problem?" asked the instructor, looking around. Many people raised their hands.

"I just guessed," said one woman. "I estimated that ¾ of my grocery store bills were spent on food and ¼ on household supplies. Is that okay?"

"Sure," responded the instructor encouragingly. "Just make the best guess you can. Don't let this problem overwhelm you. Remember, if you are over the target in one category and under in another, that's just fine.

"The next category is medical expenses. This does not include your health insurance premium. Remember, we subtracted that from the initial calculation of net income. For most people, medical expenses will be about 3% of net income."

"What if you don't have health insurance through your employer?" asked another woman. "If you have private health insurance, do those premiums go in medical expenses?"

"No," answered the instructor, "you should deduct your health insurance premiums from net income regardless of whether your insurance is provided by your employer or not. The medical expenses that belong in this category include costs over and above your insurance such as deductibles and co-pays or uninsured medical expenses such as eyeglasses or dental work.

"There's not much we can do about that category, either, is there?"

"No, there isn't. Financial crises are often precipitated by gigantic medical bills. That is why health insurance is a must. You need to have adequate insurance. We subtract it in the calculation of net income because we don't want you to even think about spending money on anything else before you have paid for your health insurance.

"Even with health insurance, your portion of your medical expenses can, on occasion, substantially exceed 3% of your net income. We'll discuss that more later when we talk about preparing for and avoiding financial crises. For now, determine what you normally spend on medical expenses. If you spend more than 3%, you will have to find the savings in another category.

"The final category is miscellaneous expenses. These average 2% of net income. They are the odds and ends that don't really fit in another category. Most of the time they are minor but occasionally someone will have a large expense that doesn't fit anywhere else. Did anyone have that happen?"

"I did," said one man. "My children go to private schools. School tuition didn't seem to belong in any of your categories, so I put it in miscellaneous."

"That's the one that comes up most often," agreed the instructor. "It's not a regular category because most people have no expense, as their children attend public schools. But for people whose children attend private schools, tuition is a major expense."

"So what do we do?"

"Keeping the cost in miscellaneous is fine. The important point is that, if miscellaneous for you is 10% of net income because of the cost of private tuition, you need to spend correspondingly less in all the other categories."

Another man seemed unconvinced. "I understand that most people don't have to pay for private grammar schools, but what about college? Don't almost all of us have to pay for college tuition?"

"You sure do," said the instructor, jumping to his feet. "But for most of your lives, you'll spend nothing on college, then the kids turn 18 and – wow – the tuition bills hit! That's why we don't treat college tuition as an annual expense; instead, we treat it as something you save for."

He turned to the flip chart and wrote the target percentages in for each category, then totaled them.

Worksheet 2-2
Target Expense Levels as a Percent of Net Income

Housing	35%
Transportation	15%
Food	14%
Entertainment	6%
Household Furnishings	5%
Clothing	5%
Household/Personal	5%
Medical Expenses	3%
Miscellaneous	2%
Total	**90%**

He then wrote on the flip chart:

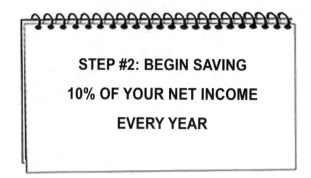

STEP #2: BEGIN SAVING

10% OF YOUR NET INCOME

EVERY YEAR

Eric spoke up: "So, if we spend at the target percentage for each category, we will spend 90% of our net income, and that will leave us 10% to save?"

"Why 10%?" asked Mark. "Does everyone need to save 10%?

The instructor answered, "As a general rule, 10% is a good savings target. Later in the seminar we will help you be more specific about your savings target. Some of you may want to save more than 10% so that you can retire at a certain age or so you can send your children to private colleges. You may need to save 15% or more of your net income to achieve those goals. For now, though, we will stick to 10% as a nice round savings target that will be adequate for most people.

"Before taking a break, we need to define two terms we will use frequently in this seminar, Saving and Investing. By Saving, we mean spending less than you earn. If your net income is $100,000 and you spend $90,000, you have Saved $10,000. You have Saved 10% of your net income. When we discuss Investing, we will be discussing what you do with the money you Save. You can Invest by buying stocks, bonds, real estate, money market funds, or simply by putting your money in the bank. Also, as you'll see after the break, you can Invest your money by repaying your existing debts.

"Investments all have a rate of return. The rate of return measures how much more money you have at the end of a year because you made the Investment. For example, if you bought a bond that paid an interest rate of 3%, your rate of return is 3%."

Looking around the room, the instructor could tell everyone needed a rest. They had covered a lot of information quickly. "Take a ten minute break," he said. "When you come back, we'll talk about debt."

CHAPTER THREE

Paying Off Debt

W hen everyone returned from the break, they found a new step written on the flip chart. It said:

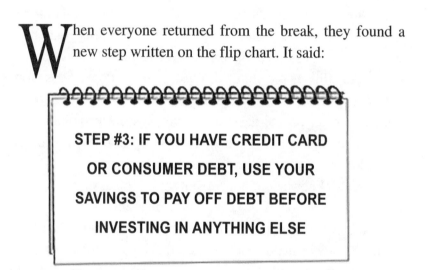

STEP #3: IF YOU HAVE CREDIT CARD

OR CONSUMER DEBT, USE YOUR

SAVINGS TO PAY OFF DEBT BEFORE

INVESTING IN ANYTHING ELSE

"What do you think about step #3?" asked the instructor, when everyone was seated.

"I'm not sure what you mean," said one woman. "Are you telling us not to invest any money until we have paid off our debt? What about contributing to our 401(k) fund?

"I don't agree with that, if that's what you mean," said Mark sharply. "My 401(k) is a huge part of my retirement savings. If I stopped putting money into my 401(k), how will I ever be able to retire?"

Another man chimed in, too: "I have always heard that the first thing you do is contribute to your 401(k). Otherwise, if you pay all your bills first, there will be nothing left for you to save. Don't we need to save for retirement?"

Joe listened to the chorus. He, too, felt thrown by Step #3. It contradicted so much of what he had heard over and over again. But something rang true. He thought about his job at the bank, and it clicked for him. He proposed, "I think I know what he's getting at. If we are borrowing on credit cards at the same time we are contributing to our 401(k), essentially, we are using borrowed money to make those contributions. That's like what we do at the bank. We borrow money from depositors and invest that money by loaning it to people on their credit cards. Our profits come because we pay our depositors a much lower interest rate than we charge on the credit cards. If someone borrows on a credit card, he is paying a very high interest rate. When he invests that money, he will probably get a lower rate of return, so he'd have a loss instead of a profit."

Andrea agreed with that. "My credit card rates are ridiculous, that's for sure. Some of them are over 15%."

"I don't know about you all, but my 401(k) is down, not up. My rate of return on that is negative," added another man.

People nodded in agreement with that comment. The last few years the stock market had produced far more losses than gains. People were worried about their retirement funds. But they didn't seem convinced yet that not contributing to their 401(k) would solve that problem.

The instructor decided to try to move the direction forward. "Joe hit the nail on the head. You will pay far more interest on credit card and consumer debt than you can normally expect to earn on any investment. I want to show this to you mathematically. There are going to be times when common sense can only take us so far, and we need to use math to demonstrate a point. Some people have a bit of a math phobia. Don't worry, the math we need is pretty simple most of the time. I call these *Let's Do the Math* examples. I'll write the calculation on the flip chart and talk you through it.

LET'S DO THE MATH	
Credit Card Balance on 1/1	$1,000
Interest rate	15%
Credit Card Balance on 12/31	**$1,150**
Savings on 1/1	$1,000
Expected stock market return	10%
Value of stock portfolio on 12/31	**$1,100**
Increased credit card debt	$ 150
Increased value of stock's owned	$ 100
Change in household net worth	**$ - 50**

"Suppose you have a balance of $1,000 on a credit card that has a 15% interest rate. In a year, if you made no payments, you would owe $1,150. Now, also suppose you have saved $1,000, and you must decide how to invest it. Using that $1,000 to pay off the credit card balance guarantees you a rate of return of 15%. Do you see why? You are turning $1,000 today into $1,150 in a year by eliminating the $1,150 you would owe your credit card company at the end of a year.

No other investment comes close to that rate of return. If instead of paying off the credit card you put the money in the stock market, and the market went up 10% over the next year (which is about average for the market), you would have $1,100 in stock. If you sold the stock at that time and used the proceeds to pay off your credit card debt, you would not be able to pay it off entirely; you'd still owe $50. Choosing to invest in stocks instead of paying off your debt would have reduced your household's net worth by $50 for that one year. The longer you continue to borrow on credit cards in order to invest, the more your debt will grow faster than your investment."

"Does this mean we have to pay off all our debts before we invest any money? What about mortgages on our house?

"Or student loans?"

"Or home equity loans?"

"Good," said the instructor, "now that we understand the reasons behind Step #3, let's discuss the exceptions to it. Can you think of some common sense reasons that we would not want to pay off our debt?"

"If we have very low interest loans," Joe suggested.

"Right," answered the instructor. "The point of Step #3 is that borrowing on credit cards to invest in something else normally will cost you a lot of money. However, if you have a mortgage, a home equity loan, a student loan, or some other debt with a low interest rate, repaying the loan may be less urgent. Generally speaking, if you are paying more than 5% or 6% on your debt, you are better off repaying the debt before you begin investing."

"You're not taking account of the employer match or the tax savings in a 401(k)," argued Mark. "If you used them in your calculation, the 401(k) might win even if your credit card rates are higher."

"It might," acknowledged the instructor. "But keep two things in mind. One, the interest you pay on the credit card is a sure thing. The rate of return on the 401(k) investment, especially in the short term, is not. Two, the credit card debt can cause you real problems now, and you won't be able to access your 401(k) money to help. As long as your credit card debt is at a manageable level of no more than 5% of your net income, investing in your 401(k) up to the amount matched by your employer may be fine. In general, though, you should think of paying off credit card debt as a prerequisite to investing in a 401(k) or anything else."

"What about keeping a rainy day fund in a savings account?" asked Andrea. "Shouldn't we do that before paying off our debt?"

"That depends on a number of things," said the instructor. If you are worried that you are about to lose your job, or that for some reason you can get credit now but may not be able to in the future, stockpiling cash makes sense.

"Under normal circumstances, I don't like the idea. Having a lot of credit card debt puts extra financial pressure on you as the balances rise. Keeping your debt low gives you more flexibility to add debt when you really need it. Having 25% of your net income in a savings account as a "rainy day fund" and the same amount as a credit card balance is a losing proposition over the long run."

The instructor paused. He was anxious to teach the group how to pay off their debt, but he couldn't push them too soon. "Are you all with me? If so, let's move on to the mechanics of getting yourself out of debt."

Joe "got" it, maybe better than the others did. His bank training helped him intuitively understand the damage done by borrowing at high rates and investing at low ones. Thinking about the past year, he wondered how he went so astray. He'd run up $20,000 in credit card debt at the same time he'd contributed $6,000 to his 401(k). The 401(k) contributions had been a conscious decision, made way back when he filled out his initial employment paperwork. Not only did it seem like the right thing at the time, Joe had felt a sense of pride in his foresight, setting aside a substantial sum for his retirement while still only 22 years old.

By contrast, there was nothing conscious about running up all that debt. It simply happened, the consequence of a sequence of unrelated decisions. In fact, until recently, he didn't even realize the total amount of debt he'd accumulated. Now that he understood his predicament, he felt determined to right his financial ship. He sat upright in his hard seat, eager for the discussion about paying down debt to begin.

The instructor began, "The program for paying down debt is quite simple. If you have read books or articles on personal finance, you likely have heard something similar. The reason everyone tells you roughly the same thing about how to pay off debt is that it works. I will go over the program step by step. Then, for your homework assignment before next session, I want you to put this program in action with your own debts.

"First, adjust your expenditure budget based on the discussion we had earlier. Make sure you get your expenditures down to no more than 90% of your net income. If you can spend less, you should, at least until your debt is close to zero.

"Second, determine if you have any savings that you can use to immediately pay down debt. If your money is tied up in a 401(k), IRA, Coverdell College Savings Account, or some other account that has a withdrawal penalty, leave it there. But if you have access to it without penalty, use as much as possible to immediately pay down your debt.

"Third, list all your remaining debts, including the interest rate, the current balance, and the minimum monthly payment.

"Fourth, determine to what extent you can shift your balances to the lower rate cards. You will need to check your paperwork or call the issuer to determine their rules regarding balance transfers and the fees they will charge.

"Fifth, investigate opening one or more new credit card accounts that offer teaser rates on balance transfers. There are many good internet sources for finding information about these cards. One of the best is www.creditcards.com. Depending on your credit score, you may be able considerably reduce your interest rate by transferring your high rate balances to a new card.

"Won't those teaser rates skyrocket after a few months?" one man asked.

"You do need to be careful with cards with teaser rates, but used correctly, they can be very helpful. First, if you are already paying a high rate, getting even six months or a year out of a teaser rate is better than nothing. Second, you may be able to find another card with a teaser rate after the first time period expires."

"Won't the credit card companies eventually stop offering you these teasers?"

"Eventually, they probably will. But if you follow this program your debt may be nearly or fully paid off by the time they do.

"Sixth, once you have shifted as much of your balances as possible to lower rate cards, you can develop a pay off order. In general, you want to pay off the highest rate card first, then the second highest rate card, then the third, etc. It also helps if you prioritize a low balance card first.

"Seventh, execute the pay off plan. Pay the minimum on all the cards except for the first card in the pay off order. Apply as much money as you can to paying off that first card. As soon as it is paid off, shift all the money that was devoted to the first card to the second card in the order. Do you see how that will boost the speed at which the second one gets paid off? Once the second one is paid off, shift all the money that was devoted to the second card to the third card in the order. Continue doing this until you have paid off all your credit cards.

"If you follow this program," asked Andrea, "how long does it usually take to pay off your debt?

"Probably less time than you might think. It depends upon the ratio of your debt to your net income. Suppose, after using any excess savings to pay down debt, you are still left with debt that is 25% of your net income. If you save 10% of your net income, your debt is 2.5 times your annual savings. If there were no interest charges, you could pay it off in 2.5 years. Depending on the interest rates on your cards, it will probably take you about three years to pay off all the debt.

"Now, if you really tighten your budget, and save 15% of your net income, your debt will only be 1.67 times your annual savings. In this case, it will only take you about two years to pay off your debt."

"It looks like we've got a lot of work to do," said Sally. For perhaps the first time in the session, there was no debate. Certainly not from Joe, who was almost out the door by the time the rest of the group was out of their seats. He was already thinking about his budget, his credit cards, and how, if he really pushed himself, he could cut his spending enough to pay off his debt and get his finances back in order before it was too late.

Save for Short-Term Goals

Beginning to Save

When Joe arrived at the seminar for the second session, the volume of conversation had notably increased. The participants clustered into threes and fours, chattering animatedly about their successes and failures with the homework assignment. Joe waved at Eric and Sally, who were already talking to Andrea, the single mother of a ten year old daughter.

Joe picked up the conversation with Sally in mid-sentence: "We cut our budget as much as we could. It is so hard, with our mortgage and two car payments, so much of our spending is locked in. The payment on both our cars alone eat up the whole Transportation Budget," Sally complained.

"My biggest problem is housing," said Andrea. I just bought a house a few months ago, and I am spending over 40% of my net income on housing and I can't lower it. I had to cut everything else deeply to get down to 90%."

"So did we," said Eric. It's going to take us more than three years just to pay off our debts. And that doesn't even leave room to save money to move to a new house. We're spending all this money on our cars, and it's not even something we care much about. Plus, as soon as we're done paying off the debt in three years, it will just about be time to buy new cars and then the whole thing will start all over again."

Joe, listening to the conversation, felt lucky. Though in the prior year he'd spent well over 100% of his net income, by vigilantly examining his budget, he had uncovered a variety of savings opportunities. Until last week, he didn't know what he could afford. Now he knew. By taking some significant steps such as moving to a less expensive apartment and trading in his Honda SUV for a more fuel efficient and less expensive car, he worked his budget down to about 85% of his net income. Following through on his plan, he would be debt free in just over two years.

Sally's voice interrupted his thoughts. "Moving is still a major objective for us, but I don't know how we'll ever afford it. We can't save any money for it, and we don't know if we've got any equity in our house the way the market is today."

"I think today's session is supposed to cover buying a house. I hope it helps," Eric added wistfully.

As if on cue, the instructor asked everyone to take their seats. "Today we will discuss what to do with your savings once you have paid off your debt. Imagine you are at that date, hopefully not too far in the future, when you have paid off your debt, and you are able to begin to use your savings to build up assets. What will you be saving for?"

The answers came fast and furious. Everyone had something they were anxious to save for. "My kids' college education. That's my main focus. I have three children, and with what college costs, I know I'm going to need to have a fortune saved," said one woman.

"Retirement," said another man. "I have kids, too, but they are working hard to save for their own college education. I have been working since I was sixteen years old, and I'm getting tired. I'd like to see a light at the end of the tunnel."

"Our focus is a house," said Sally, with one eye on Eric and the other on the rest of the group. "We want to save for retirement, too, and we definitely need to save for our children's college education. There are so many things to save for, it's hard to know where to begin."

"Why do you need to begin anywhere?" asked Andrea. "Why can't you just save money without it being for anything specific? I know I am going to need money for retirement, and for college, and for a house, and for who knows what else. But when I save money, I just save it without it being "for" something. Then, whenever I need it, I can take my money out of savings."

"I like that idea," agreed another man. What's the point of forcing yourself to decide now what you're saving for? You never know what the future holds."

"That's certainly true," offered the instructor. Scanning the class, he asked, "Do you all prefer the idea of just saving in general?

"I prefer to save for something specific," said one man. "It's more motivating, so it helps me save. If I have a goal, I can track how close I am to achieving that goal."

"You're not alone," said the instructor. "Many people find it helpful to keep separate "accounts" for each of their goals. I call them Funds. You may have a Retirement Fund, a College Fund, and a Home Fund, as well as some others."

"Can you use the money from one Fund for something else?" asked one man.

"Sure," said the instructor, "it's still your money. The Funds just help you improve your financial planning. You determine a dollar amount that is each Fund's goal. When the fund reaches the goal, you can use the money in the fund for whatever the fund was established to achieve: buy a house, retire, whatever."

Andrea didn't buy it. "That just doesn't seem realistic. Who knows how much money you are going to need to retire? I'm 40 years old. It will be at least 25 years before I retire. How much money do I have to save? It's impossible to know. I think you're kidding yourself if you think you can predict that now."

Her argument made sense. The group turned to the instructor, waiting for his response. He had built up some credibility in the first session, but the general skepticism of the participants hadn't been fully extinguished, and this cogent undermining of his Fund concept seemed to rekindle it.

"You bring up some excellent points," began the instructor. "Before dealing with them directly, I need to introduce a distinction between two basic categories of savings goals: long-term goals and short-term goals. Long-term goals are the objectives that usually require us to save for ten or more years. The two main long term goals are college education and retirement.

"Short-term goals are the objectives that usually require only a few years of saving. The two main short-term goals are buying a house and buying a car. Is everyone with me so far?"

They all seemed to be, so he continued. "Let's discuss some differences between short-term and long-term goals. Andrea made a very strong case about the difficulty of setting a goal for your Retirement Fund. But suppose you have a short-term goal such as buying a car. Will it be as hard to set that goal?"

"What is the goal? Is it just the down payment or is it the whole car?" asked Eric.

"The whole car," answered the instructor. "Assume your objective is to save enough to pay cash for a car. How hard is it to set a goal?

"Not very hard," offered Joe. You can go online and see exactly what you need to pay for any car you want."

"Right. You can be very precise with your goal for your Auto Fund. Your House Fund may be a little less precise, but it's still relatively easy to set a goal. For short-term goals, and by that I primarily mean the Auto Fund and the Home Fund, with a little research you can set a good target."

"That makes sense," said one man. "But what do you do for long-term objectives?"

"Long-term objectives are more complicated. You can still set goals – in fact, having a roadmap for your long-term objectives is especially important. We'll discuss how to set them in a couple weeks. Right now, let's enjoy the simplicity of saving for short-term goals.

"Once you have a specific dollar goal for your Fund, calculate how much you can contribute to the Fund each month. If you are saving for only one goal at a time, and your debts are paid off, the amount you can contribute to the Fund is the full difference between your net income and your total expenditures, your Annual Savings.'"

Andrea continued to resist. "Who can save for one thing at a time? We all have lots of things we need to save for."

"Humor me for a minute," requested the instructor. "We will eventually have a discussion on how to allocate your savings dollars. For now, assume all your Annual Savings are going into your Auto Fund. Since you have a specific dollar goal, and you know how much you'll save each month, you can calculate an estimated date for achieving your goal. Do you see how you are layering certainty onto your financial future? You already have clarity into how long you will need to repay your debts. You now have similar clarity into how long you will need to achieve your short-term objectives."

"Only if you continue to assume that you ignore your long-term objectives," countered Andrea, still skeptical. "If you are realistic and accept that you need to save money for many things at once, I don't think you have as much clarity as you say."

"You're right, Andrea. Saving for many things at once tends to reduce clarity. And clarity is very beneficial. I want to make a general statement regarding the prioritization of different goals. We began the seminar last week discussing debt. We made a point of the importance of paying off debt before beginning to save for anything else. Now I'll follow that up."

He turned to the flip chart next to him, and wrote:

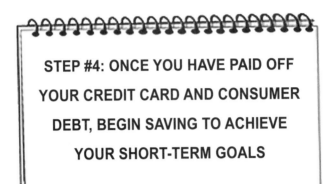

STEP #4: ONCE YOU HAVE PAID OFF YOUR CREDIT CARD AND CONSUMER DEBT, BEGIN SAVING TO ACHIEVE YOUR SHORT-TERM GOALS

"Are you telling us you still don't want us putting money into our 401(k)? You've got to be kidding!" Mark was flabbergasted. "I was just beginning to accept your argument about the debt, but now I am wondering again. How can we build up enough money in our retirement accounts if we need to do all these other things first?"

"Not just retirement, what about college?" added Andrea. "If we wait until all these other goals are met and our debt is paid off, our kids will be college age, and we won't have saved anything."

The instructor appeared calm. He expected this response from the group. He also knew their concerns were valid. "Remember the basic concept. Paying high-interest consumer and credit card debt sets you back faster than your investments can grow. It makes you less wealthy, puts you at risk for financial crises, and inhibits your ability to achieve your goals.

"Prioritizing short-term savings goals builds on that premise. Once you pull yourself out of debt, you must stay out of debt. The inability to afford your inevitable short-term purchases can sink you back into debt. *By saving for your big purchases before you make them, you can avoid that fate.* If, for example, you accumulate enough money in your Auto Fund to buy your car with cash, you will avoid the need to take out an auto loan."

"That makes sense, but it doesn't address Andrea's question about college," said one man. "If you don't have savings for college, you're going to need to go into debt to pay the tuition bills."

"That's a very good point," accepted the instructor. "At some point, college switches from being a long-term goal to a short-term goal. If your child is a junior in high school, it hardly makes sense to think of college as being way out in the future. It may be a long term goal when your child is born, but at some point it becomes a short-term goal.

"I know what you are learning is unsettling. You don't need to trust me that it is right. I will prove it to you over the course of the seminar. But, for now, I do need you to trust me that I will not ignore your long-term objectives. We will attend to them eventually. We simply need to deal with the short-term objectives first.

"Let's break for a few minutes. During the rest of today's session, we will discuss how to save so that you can achieve your short-term objectives."

CHAPTER FIVE

The Auto Fund

A s everyone reassembled in their seats after the break, the instructor began the discussion. "For the next part of this session we will discuss the Auto Fund. Remember, we divided savings objectives into two categories, long-term objectives and short-term objectives. I put Step #4 on the board, which says that after repaying your consumer and credit card debt, you prioritize saving to achieve your short-term objectives, principally autos and homes. For most people, autos are priority number one, and homes are priority number two."

"Why is that?" asked Sally. "It seems to me that a home is a more important and more expensive expenditure. Shouldn't it be a higher priority?"

"By higher priority," answered the instructor, "I don't mean more important. I mean that you save for it *first*. I am talking about sequence. You save money for an auto first – assuming you need a car – for two reasons: one, auto debt is destructive debt, whereas home mortgages, which have lower interest rates and are tax deductible, are not. Two, if you cannot yet afford to buy a home, renting is a good option. No similar option exists for cars."

"What about leasing?" asked another participant. "Isn't leasing a car like renting a house? I have always leased my cars, because I can afford a better car for the same monthly payment. Isn't that a good deal?"

"No," answered the instructor, "leasing is the worst deal of all. Here's why. First, the lower monthly payment encourages you to choose a more expensive car than you can really afford. Second, leasing is worse than buying using an auto loan because you don't build up equity in your car when you lease. Suppose you buy a car that you plan to keep for four years. You take out a loan with a four year term. At the end of four years, you will have paid off the entire loan, and you will own the car. When you buy a new car at that point, you can trade in your current car, and you will probably receive about 55-60% of the amount you originally paid for the car.

"On the other hand, if you had leased the car for four years, at the end of the four years the car would go back to the dealer, and at best you would receive nothing. At worst, you may have to pay penalties if you have exceeded your mileage limit or if you have damaged in the car. When you buy your next car, instead of having substantial value in your trade-in, you will be starting from scratch.

"The third problem with leasing is that you pay the same high interest rate you would pay if you had a loan on your car. The interest rate is built into the lease payments. Because the interest rate is hidden, and it is hard for you to determine exactly what rate you are paying, you can be certain you are not "getting a deal" on the interest rate.

"The fourth problem with leasing is reduced flexibility. You cannot easily terminate a lease before it expires. Suppose you lose your job and you need to trade down to a less expensive car. It is much easier if you own your car than if you have leased it. Or, suppose you save effectively and want to pay off high-interest debt. Paying off an auto loan early is much easier than paying off a lease early. Leases, in general, reduce your flexibility. Avoiding leases is a firm recommendation."

The instructor paused to give everyone a chance to think through the discussion. "Now," said the instructor, "let's explore the problem with auto loans. Say you have worked hard for the last couple years monitoring your budget and paying off all your credit card and previous auto debt. You now own your car debt free. That's great, but eventually you will need to replace the car. If you take out a new loan when you make the purchase, you will have gone back into debt. You will be back to paying a high rate of interest, reducing your wealth and inhibiting your ability to accomplish all your other financial goals."

"That's not always the case," commented one man. "Just like you said before, sometimes you can buy a car with a very low interest loan. Isn't that a good option?"

The instructor surveyed the group. "What do you all think? If the manufacturer is offering a special low interest loan, should you take it?"

No one spoke up at first. Remembering last week's conversation, in which he told them not to pay off a low interest auto loan early, it seemed to follow that taking out such a loan must be a good idea. Still they had the sense that something was wrong with that choice.

"Can't you usually get a rebate if you pass up the low-interest loan?" offered Joe.

"Exactly," said the instructor. He turned to the flip chart and wrote:

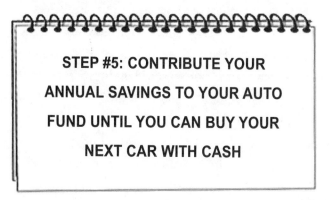

STEP #5: CONTRIBUTE YOUR ANNUAL SAVINGS TO YOUR AUTO FUND UNTIL YOU CAN BUY YOUR NEXT CAR WITH CASH

He continued: "The low or zero interest loan is almost never a good deal when you consider you are paying a higher price for the car than you would if you pass up the loan offer. Paying cash will nearly always buy you the same car at a better price. The auto loan, even a very low interest loan, is a bad deal. You will substantially increase your wealth over your lifetime by paying all cash each time you purchase a car. Few people do this because cars are expensive. If you don't make it a priority, you will never be in a position to do it. However, once you pay cash for your first car, buying each subsequent car with cash becomes easy. If you choose, you can even buy progressively more expensive cars each time without increasing the percentage of your net income devoted to Transportation Expense."

The class was intrigued. Sally spoke for her fellow classmates, "I sure would like to hear how you do this. We are spending so much on our car payments now it is getting in the way of everything else we want to do. How do we go from paying off our loans on two cars to owning two cars?"

"I'm going to show you how," answered the instructor. "Flash forward to that future date when you will have repaid all your credit card and consumer debts, including all your existing auto debt. Because you are debt free, you can begin contributing your entire Annual Savings to your Auto Fund. In addition, because you have no auto loans, you can devote some of your Transportation Budget toward filling up your Auto Fund. Recall that the target amount of Transportation Expense is 15% of net income. Normally, about 6% of that goes toward auto purchases, leaving the other 9% for gas, insurance, repairs and maintenance, public transportation, and other expenses. Adding that 6% to your Annual Savings of at least 10%, you can put 16% of your net income into your Auto Fund."

"I still think that's unrealistic. You're assuming we don't save for anything else. We all have lots of other things to save for, we can't put all our savings toward our cars," commented Mark a bit acidly.

"In the long run you obviously can't but for a few years it is fine. Let's do the math. Suppose you want to buy a $15,000 car and your net income is $50,000. By putting 16% of your net income into your Auto Fund, you will contribute $8,000 per year. In just under two years, you will be able to buy your car. After that you will never need to use your Annual Savings toward your auto fund again! By focusing all your Annual Savings into your Auto Fund for that brief, two year period, you will be able to pay cash for your cars for the rest of your life."

"That sounds great, but I don't get it. Won't you still need to save each time it is time to buy a new car?" asked Sally.

"Sure, you'll need to save, but you won't need to use your Annual Savings," explained the instructor. "You will be able to use the 6% of your Transportation Expense to contribute to your Auto Fund each year. That's all you will ever need. Continue with our example of a family with a net income of $50,000 per year. Six percent of that is $3,000. This family has just purchased a car for $15,000. Every year going forward, they will contribute $3,000 into their Auto Fund without using their Annual Savings and they will still have 10% of their net income to save for whatever they choose.

"Let's assume the car they just bought will last five years before they sell it. After five years, they will have put $15,000 into the Auto Fund. The 5-year old car will be worth about 50% of what they paid for it, or $7,500. By combining the trade-in value with the savings in the Auto Fund, they will be able to pay cash for a new car with a price of $22,500."

"This family has within the space of five years traded up from a $15,000 car to a $22,500 car without doing anything but maintaining a standard Transportation Expenditure. If they continue the process again over the next five years, they will again contribute $15,000 to the Auto Fund during that time span. The trade-in value this time will be $11,250 – half of $22,500, so they can buy a new car worth $26,250. Again, they can "trade up" without using any of their Annual Savings which has now been freed up for other purposes."

LET'S DO THE MATH

1st All-Cash Car Purchase

Net Income	$50,000
Annual Contribution Rate to Auto Fund	16%
Annual Auto Fund Contribution	$8,000
Cost of Auto	$15,000
Time Required Prior to Purchase	**1 year, 11 months**

2nd All-Cash Car Purchase

Annual Contribution Rate to Auto Fund	6%
Annual Auto Fund Contribution	$3,000
Amount in Auto Fund after 5 years	$15,000
Value of Owned Car after 5 years	$7,500
Total Amount Available to Purchase 2nd Car	**$22,500**

3rd All-Cash Car Purchase

Annual Contribution Rate to Auto Fund	6%
Annual Auto Fund Contribution	$3,000
Amount in Auto Fund after 5 years	$15,000
Value of Owned Car after 5 years	$11,250
Total Amount Available to Purchase 3rd Car	**$26,250**

"It looks like you might even be underestimating what they'll be able to buy," added Joe. You are assuming they continue to make $50,000 forever. But if they get raises over time, their net income will grow, and instead of contributing $3,000 per year into their Auto Fund they could contribute more without exceeding their Transportation Budget."

"That's certainly true. This technique allows you to continually trade your cars in for more expensive cars throughout your lifetime without either increasing your income or spending a higher percentage of your income on cars. That is the magic of buying cars with cash instead of debt. That is why you prioritize your Auto Fund first."

"I'm not sure I care about increasing the value of my car over my life," commented Andrea, who seemed to be coming around to the idea of prioritizing the Auto Fund by now. "I drive a Ford Focus now and I'd be happy to drive the same car forever. I like it, and it is perfectly fine for my lifestyle. Would I be able to spend less and less of my money on cars as I get older?"

"You can certainly spend less than 6% of net income. Let's go back to the example. If you wanted to continually pay $15,000 for each new car, and after five years trade in the old car for $7,500, you would need to save $7,500 every five years. That means instead of contributing $3,000 per year, you would only need to contribute $1,500 a year to your Auto Fund. Instead of contributing 6% of your net income, you would contribute 3% of your net income. You would forever have an additional 3% of your net income to either spend in another area or to devote to savings."

"Three percent doesn't sound like much," said one man. "I'm not sure I'd like the idea of driving a $15,000 car my whole life just to save three percent."

"After what I just went through to cut three percent out of my budget, I don't agree that it isn't much," retorted Andrea. "Getting my spending down from 93% to 90% of net income was really hard."

"That three percent would really add up over time," Eric added. "If you saved an extra three percent a year, wouldn't that have a big impact eventually?"

"It sure would," said the instructor. "This is a great time to do a little more math. Eric, let's use you and Sally as an example. About how much is your and Sally's net income?"

Eric hesitated. It wasn't something he typically announced in front of a large group. The instructor, sensing his hesitation, encouraged him. "Remember, we are going to talk openly about finances here. We need to bring our real issues out into the open, so we can develop real solutions. You will understand better if you use real numbers."

"Our net income is about $100,000," Eric finally said.

"Good. How old are you?"

"I'm thirty years old, and so is Sally."

"Okay," said the instructor to the whole group. "Eric's family has net income of $100,000 per year. Suppose they decide not to spend 6% of their net income on autos; instead, they will spend only 3%. They will put the additional $3,000 each year into your 401(k)."

"Hallelujah!" exclaimed Mark. For the first time that day, the class laughed.

The instructor, smiling, continued. "Eric and Sally are 30 years old and will continue saving this additional $3,000 per year for the next 37 years, until they are age 67 and ready to retire. Assume also that over that period of time they have a rate of return of 9.5% on the investments in their 401(k), which is approximately the historical market average. When they retire, they will have about $875,000 extra in their retirement account! That three percent per year additional savings turns into $875,000."

LET'S DO THE MATH

Family Net Income	$100,000
Standard Auto Expense	6%
Standard Auto Fund Contribution	$6,000
Reduced Auto Expense	3%
Reduced Auto Fund Contribution	$3,000
Additional 401k Contribution	$3,000
Number of Years	37
Compound annual rate of return	9.5%
Increased size of 401k fund after 35 years	**$875,657**

"Wow." Eric and sally looked at each other and at the numbers. "That's a huge number."

The instructor drove the point home. "While three percent of net income may not seem like much, over your lifetime it really does matter. If cars are important to you, by all means spend up to your six percent target. But if you can be satisfied with a less expensive car, you can really benefit from spending less."

Sally was very excited. She wanted to be sure she understood. "I see we should try to save that extra 3% if we can. Exactly how do we do it? Plus, we have two cars. Does that matter? How do we decide how much to spend on each car?"

"Let's do the math step by step," answered the instructor. "The first all-cash purchase is a little different than subsequent purchases. The sooner you can make your first all-cash purchase, the better. Recall that you will be contributing around 16% of net income to your Auto Fund. You don't want to do this for too long. With no money left to save for anything else, all your other objectives are on hold. Also, you will probably have been driving your current cars for a while when you begin contributing to your Auto Fund, because you've been paying off all your debt for the last few years. Don't buy a clunker you'll need to replace in two years; you need a car that will last you five years or more. But for that first all-cash purchase, *determine the least expensive car you can live with for the next five years, and buy that one as soon as you can afford it.* You will have ample time to upgrade your cars over the years.

"After you've bought your first all-cash auto, use the following formula to determine what you can spend on future auto purchases: first, calculate the expected trade-in value of the car you own. As a rule, cars lose about 17.5% of their value after one year and 10% of their value all future years. Estimate how long you plan to keep your current car and what it will be worth as a trade-in. Second, decide how much of your Transportation Budget you plan to contribute to your Auto Fund each year. The standard amount is about 6%. If you want to reduce that to 3%, use that amount. Multiply 3% by your net income to determine how much money you will put in your Auto Fund each year. Next, multiply that number by the number of years you plan to keep your cars, then divide by the number of cars in your family. The answer will be the amount from the Auto Fund available for each car. Finally, add the Auto Fund amount to the trade-in value. The sum is the amount you will be able to spend on your next car."

LET'S DO THE MATH

Average Price of Current Cars	$15,000
Average Resale Value after 5 years	$7,500
Income	$100,000
Rate of Auto Fund Contribution	x 3%
Annual Contribution	$3,000
Years Autos will be kept	x 5
Total Contribution between Purchases	$15,000
Number of Cars in Family	÷ 2
Amount per Car	$7,500
Average Resale Value after 5 years	+ $7,500
Target Price of each New Car	**$15,000**

"What if that amount isn't enough to buy the car you want?" asked Eric.

"Now you are in a position to make an educated choice, to balance your desire for a better car against enhancing your ability to save for other goals. If you had planned to contribute only 3% of net income to your Auto Fund, but that doesn't allow you to buy your desired car, you must decide whether to increase your contribution rate or settle for a less expensive car."

Eric and Sally seemed quite pleased. An issue which had been weighing heavily on them, though not yet resolved, had been clarified. They knew what to do when they went home from the session.

"Let's take another break," suggested the instructor. "Our next subject is the Home Fund."

CHAPTER SIX

The Home Fund

As the group returned from the break, the instructor encouraged them to quickly take their seats. "We have lots of material to cover," he said. "And I suspect that you will have plenty of concerns about it. Much of this evening's material will contradict some of your deeply ingrained assumptions."

People snapped to attention. If the instructor prefaced the Home Fund discussion by preparing them for unexpected advice, he would not likely disappoint them.

"A little review," he began. "The first step for nearly everyone is paying off your credit card and consumer debt. The second step is buying your cars with cash. Now, imagine that time in the future when you have paid off your debt and purchased your car or cars with cash. You no longer need to devote your Annual Savings to paying off debt or to your Auto Fund. If you do not yet own a home, you will probably want to begin contributing some or all of your Annual Savings into your Home Fund."

"What if you are already a homeowner?" asked about three participants at once. As the group spanned the entire spectrum of ages, more than half of them appeared to already own a home.

"Most people, if they already own a home," answered the instructor, "won't need to create a Home Fund."

"What if you want to move to a bigger house?" asked Sally. As Sally had made abundantly clear, she was very anxious to move to a larger home. "Don't you need to save for that?"

"Homeowners like you can save money toward a future home without using a Home Fund. You can use your Annual Savings to prepay your mortgage. Then, when you sell your current home, you will have more equity to roll into your new home.

"Sally, there are some extra issues to consider for people like you who already own a home, but who want to move. We'll get to them, but first let's start with the simplest situation -- someone who is currently renting. A renter must contribute his Annual Savings into a Home Fund for a number of years to accumulate the money required for the down payment and other initial costs of buying a home."

Mark was ready to jump out of his seat. "I feel like I am continually bringing this up, but I just don't get it. By the time we pay off our debt, buy a car or two, and buy a home, there won't be any time left to save for the long-term goals. It seems like you're telling us to sacrifice the long-term for the short-term."

"I know it might seem that way," replied the instructor. The notion that people must start saving for retirement as early as possible had received so much publicity that questioning it seemed unthinkable. "You must pay off your credit card and consumer debt, and if you need a car, you must buy it with cash instead of leasing it or taking out an auto loan, because these high interest rate debts actually undermine the achievement of your long-term goals more than failing to save for them does. By taking care of your short-term needs, you best position yourself to achieve your long-term goals.

"Once you are ready to contribute to the Home Fund, however, you have a little more flexibility. If you are a renter who has reached the age when you need to start saving for your long-term objectives, you may wish to split your Annual Savings between your Home Fund and your long-term objectives. Recognize that diverting savings from your Home Fund means that you will either rent for longer or you will buy a less expensive home. Does that make sense?"

Mark, who could not dispute the logic, reluctantly acquiesced, at least for the moment. The instructor resumed.

"Let's go through the process of calculating how long a renter will need to save before he can buy a home. Imagine you are currently renting but want to buy a home. Think about the main factors that impact the price of a home. Determine where you want to live, what size home you want, and any other factor that will have a major impact on the price of the home. Next, find out the average price of the homes that fit your description. You can look the prices up online, or you can ask a real estate broker to provide them. Without much difficulty, you can determine approximately how much you would have to pay if you purchased the home you want today.

Next, divide the amount you expect to pay by four. This is roughly the amount you will need to contribute to your Home Fund in order to buy that home. Most of the money in the Home Fund will be used for your down payment, which normally is 20% of the purchase price. The rest of the money in the Home Fund will cover closing costs, moving expenses, immediate upgrades, and furniture purchases that you will make when you move into your new home. Now that you know how much money you need in the Home Fund, divide that number by the amount you plan to contribute to the Home Fund each year, and you will know how long it will take before you can buy the home."

"What if you don't want to wait as long as the calculation tells you it will take?" asked one man in his mid-thirties who had been quiet until that moment.

"That's a great question," answered the instructor. "What's your name?"

"James," answered the man.

"James, the longer you are willing to wait, the more you can afford to spend on the home. Let's Do Some Math to illustrate the trade off between the amount of time before you buy a home and the cost of the home. Approximately what is your net income?

"$50,000," answered James.

"OK. Assume your Annual Savings is 10% of that, $5,000. You contribute your entire Annual Savings to your Home Fund each year. After five years you will have $25,000 in your Home Fund. Multiply that by four, and you will be able to buy a home that costs $100,000 in five years."

"$100,000 doesn't buy much of a home," James said.

"No, it doesn't. If you wanted to purchase a home that costs $140,000, you'd need $35,000 in your Home Fund. You could get to that amount by waiting two more years, which is a total of seven years," said the instructor.

LET'S DO THE MATH

Net Income	$50,000
Annual Home Fund Contribution	$5,000
Number of Years to Home Purchase	x 5
Funds Available for Home Purchase	$25,000
Multiplier	x 4
Target Price for Home Purchase	**$100,000**
New Number of Years to Home Purchase	7
Annual Home Fund Contribution	x 5,000
Funds Available for Home Purchase	$35,000
Multiplier	x 4
New Target Price for Home Purchase	**$140,000**

That prospect didn't appeal to James much. "Seven years seems a very long time to waste renting. Couldn't I put down less than 20% on the house?"

"Not anymore. A few years ago you could put nothing down, right? That's why we had a big housing bubble. Since people could buy a house with no down payment, they bought more and more expensive houses, driving the cost of housing to astronomical heights. Those kinds of loans are no longer available."

"Aren't there any exceptions? I can't imagine having to rent for seven more years," James begged.

"It's not just seven years," added Mark. "Remember, this is after paying off the credit cards and buying the cars with cash. That could easily be five years. You are telling James he has to rent for twelve years if he doesn't already own a home right now."

James looked astounded. "Oh, that can't be a good idea. How could it possibly make sense to pay rent for twelve years instead of building up equity in a home over that time?" Something didn't compute for any of the participants.

The instructor addressed the class. "I said at the beginning that you'd learn something surprising. Let's compare the economics of renting a home to the economics of buying a home. What is the primary reason owning a home is preferable to renting?"

"If you own a home you don't pay rent," said one man.

"Okay, but what's wrong with paying rent?"

"You have nothing to show for it. Every year you pay your rent, but you don't build up any ownership. The money is gone forever."

"True," said the instructor. "What if you own a home?" He gestured to the class. "I want all you homeowners to shout out some expenses you have as a homeowner that you typically would not have as a renter."

The answers came loudly and quickly. The homeowners knew well where their money went.

"Real estate taxes."

"Association dues."

"Homeowners insurance."

"Repairs and maintenance."

"Great. These costs are not insignificant. When comparing the economics of owning and renting, we can't ignore these costs. Let's Do The Math. The historical average cost to rent a home is about 1/20th, or five percent, the price of the home. A home that costs $100,000 will normally rent for about $5,000 per year. If, instead, you buy a house for $100,000 and put $20,000 down, you will have a mortgage of $80,000. Assume you get a 6%, 30 year mortgage. Your monthly payment is $479.64, so your mortgage payments are $5,755.69 per year. Add to that all the other expenses we called out, which average about 3%. That adds $3,000, so your total out of pocket costs each year are $8,755.69, close to double a renter's for the exact same property!"

"Wait a minute," said Mark. "What about the tax benefit of owning. You can deduct your mortgage and real estate taxes from your income tax bill."

"Yes," agreed the instructor, "that narrows the gap, but even for people in the highest tax bracket, renting still costs less."

LET'S DO THE MATH

Home Value	$100,000
Mortgage Amount	$80,000
Mortgage Years	30
Mortgage Interest Rate	6%
Monthly Payment	$479.64
Number of Months	12
Annual Payment	$5,756
Homeowner expense rate (includes real estate taxes, insurance association dues and or maintenance)	3%
Homeowner expenses	$3,000
Annual Homeowner Costs	$8,756
Tax Deduction[1]	$1,575
After Tax Annual Homeowner Costs	**$7,181**
Home Value	$100,000
Rental rate	5%
Rental Cost	**$5,000**

"Well, sure," said James, who did not seem ready to give up, now that he'd been engaged. "But when you rent you're not building up any ownership. When you move out of a home you rented, you get nothing. You can make a lot of money when you sell a house."

---

[1] Tax Deduction is based on 25% tax rate. Someone in the 35% tax bracket would have a deduction of $2,205, and would still have costs about $1,500 more than a renter.

"I wish I had made a lot of money when I sold my house," lamented one woman. "I thought I was going to, when I bought it. But the price went down, not up. I actually lost money."

Judging from the expressions and mumblings from the group, she was not alone. Few home owners had been spared by the Great Housing Crash of the late 2000s. "We're in the same situation," said Sally. "When we bought our house, we only planned to stay a few years. We had friends who had made money trading up houses every couple of years. They would buy a house, live there a little while, sell it for a big profit, and move to a better house. Meanwhile, we felt like we were wasting money paying rent on the same lousy apartment.

"When I was pregnant with the baby, and we needed to move anyway, we figured we'd buy a little house. It's fine for one child but not two. We planned to move when we had the second child and make a big profit like our friends had."

Sally's story struck a chord with her classmates. Many of them had friends who had made a fortune buying and selling their homes a few years ago. When the housing market stopped going up and started going down, those "fortunes" disappeared overnight.

"The instructor commented, "Home flipping seemed like a good idea a few years ago. If home values are rising very rapidly, like they were in the mid-2000s, you can make a lot of money buying and selling homes. But under normal circumstances, buying and selling a home after just a few years is a real wealth destroyer. Here is something that might surprise you." He stood up and wrote on the flip chart:

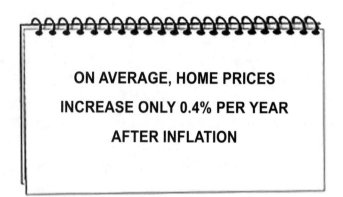

ON AVERAGE, HOME PRICES
INCREASE ONLY 0.4% PER YEAR
AFTER INFLATION

"What do you mean, 'after inflation'," asked one man.

"I mean that home prices increase, on average, only 0.4% more than inflation. For example, if inflation is 3% in a year, you would expect home prices to increase by 3.4%."

"That doesn't sound like much," said the man.

"It isn't much. It means that, most of the time, your home will be worth about the same amount, in inflation-adjusted dollars, when you sell it as it was worth when you bought it."

"Can you explain what you mean by inflation adjusted dollars?" asked another woman.

"Absolutely. This is a critical concept, one that we will come back to over and over again as we discuss various investments. Think back to 1980. If you had $1,000 in 1980, you could buy a lot more with that $1,000 than you can buy today. The U.S. government has a department called the Bureau of Labor Statistics that measures what that $1,000 can buy. It publishes a statistic called the Consumer Price Index, or CPI for short. Suppose the CPI has risen by 3% in the last year. That means that you would need $1,030 today to buy what you could have purchased with $1,000 last year.

"Sally, would you and Eric mind being our example again?"

Sally, who was very intent on finding a solution to her housing problem, agreed.

"What did you pay for your house?"

"About $200,000."

"And how long have you owned it?"

"Five years."

"Okay. Suppose in the last five years the CPI has gone up by 15% (3% each year[2]). To have the same amount of 'purchasing power' if you sell the house today that you had when you bought the house, you'd need to sell it for $230,000. Because, on average, homes rise 0.4% per year faster than the CPI, you would expect to sell the house for an extra 2% (5 years times 0.4%) more than you bought it for, or $4,000 more. That would make the total sales price $234,000, and you would have gained $4,000 in real purchasing power."

"But it's definitely not worth $234,000 today. It's not even worth $200,000 anymore," sighed Sally.

"Yes. Unfortunately, values don't always rise by the average amount, in homes or any other investment. Sometimes they rise more than average, sometimes less than average, and sometimes they fall. I suspect you are all well aware of that now. I want to show you something you are probably not aware of, at least not consciously. Suppose Sally and Eric's house actually was worth $234,000 today. Would it be okay for them to sell and move?"

The class paused. Though the answer seemed obvious, they felt unsure. Finally, one man spoke: "Why wouldn't it be? They've gained $4,000 in purchasing power, which may not be a lot, but it's better than nothing."

"You've only seen half the picture so far. Think about all the costs that go into selling one home and moving to a new one. Go ahead and shout out some of those costs and I'll write them down." The instructor went back to the flip chart.

"Brokerage fees," shouted someone.

---

[2] For simplicity, this example ignores the impact of compounding, which is trivial in this case.

"Yes, that's the biggest one. Every time you sell a house, you will pay fees to your real estate broker, usually five or six percent of the sale price."

"Closing costs on the new home purchase," called another.

"Yes. What are some of those?"

"Title fees, legal fees, appraisal fees, mortgage fees and points, and various other little fees. They can really add up."

"They sure can," agreed the instructor. "Various Closing Costs typically run between two and four percent of the cost of the new home."

"What about transfer taxes?" asked a third person. "I think I had to pay a transfer tax when I bought my last home."

"Transfer taxes vary by state and county. They can sometimes be as much as one percent of the value of the home."

"Don't forget moving costs," called a fourth. "You can spend thousands of dollars on movers, especially if you are moving to another city."

"Look at the list," said the instructor. "Brokerage fees, Closing Costs, Transfer Taxes, and Moving Expenses. You can expect to lose as much as ten percent or more of the value of your home in all the Transaction Costs of selling one home and buying another. This is especially true if your home is worth a few hundred thousand dollars or less. Even if your home is worth $1 million or more, you should still expect to lose at least 7-8% in Transaction Costs.

"Now, let's revisit Sally and Eric's predicament. I will show you that even if the value of their house had grown in value as much as they would normally expect, buying a house with a plan to move in five years into a larger house made poor financial sense. Let's Do The Math. Sally and Eric's home cost $200,000. Sally, how much was your down payment?"

"I am pretty sure it was 20%," Sally answered. She looked to Eric for confirmation. He agreed.

Table 6-1
**Transaction Costs of Selling
and Buying a Home**

Brokerage Fees	5-6%
Closing Costs	2-4%
Title Fees	
Legal Fees	
Appraisal Fees	
Mortgage Fees and Points	
Transfer Taxes	0-1%
Moving Expenses	0-2%
Total Expected Costs	7-13%

"Good. That means they put $40,000 down and have a mortgage of $160,000. Do you recall the length of the mortgage and the interest rate?"

They conferred quickly. Eric said, "It is a 30-year fixed mortgage. We think the interest rate is around six percent."

The instructor quickly punched the numbers into a calculator, and then he turned to the group. "Now, suppose they move today, five years later. Assume their home had appreciated in value by 3.4 percent per year, so they sell it for about $236,000.[3] After Transaction Costs of 10%, and repaying their mortgage, which will have about $149,000 remaining, they will have about $64,000 to put toward a down payment on a new, larger home. If they take out a new mortgage with the same terms – 30 years, $160,000, 6% interest – they will be able to buy a new house for about $224,000."

He pauses. "Does anyone see the problem here?"

---

[3] The difference between $236,392 and 234,000 is the effect of compounding.

Joe raises his hand. "I think so. They are able to buy a new house for $224,000. But the house they just sold went for $236,000. So they will actually be trading down, not up."

"Exactly!" shouted the instructor. "Even though, in this hypothetical example, their house appreciated in value by the historically average amount, after five years of paying the mortgage they have not built up enough equity to trade up to a better house. If they move they actually have to trade down."

LET'S DO THE MATH

Original Home Price	$200,000
Average Inflation Rate	3.0%
Additional Home Value Growth	+ 0.4%
Total Annual Price Appreciation	3.4%
Years in Home	5
Sale Price of Home after Fifth Year	$236,392
Original Mortgage	$160,000
Term in Years	30
Interest Rate	6%
Principal Paid after 5 Years	$11,113
Outstanding Principal	$148,887
Sale Price	$236,392
Closing Costs (at 10%)	− $23,639
Outstanding Principal	− $148,887
Down Payment on New Home	$63,866
Mortgage on New Home	+ $160,000
Total Available for New Home	$223,866
Reduced Value of New Home	**$12,526**

After giving everyone a chance to digest the numbers, the instructor continued. "Compare this outcome to renting. Had they rented a comparable house, they would have saved considerable money each year. Adding those savings to the down payment which they would have had invested over the last five years, they would be in a far better position to move to a more expensive home now."

"I don't get it," said James. "Are you telling us that we should never own a home?"

"No, certainly not, answered the instructor. "Owning a home will *eventually* beat renting if you stay in the home long enough. You've got to stay in the home more than five years, or renting makes better economic sense. In addition, there is a great benefit from the flexibility of renting. Sally, you have mentioned more than once that you would like to move but are trapped by your mortgage. Think how much less restricted your situation would be if you had rented your home instead of bought it."

"It's true," agreed Sally. "The home is a real ball and chain for us."

"Buying a home is much riskier than people have been led to believe. If you lose your job, become disabled, or lose your income for any reason, owning a home with a mortgage is a big problem. If you cannot pay your mortgage you will be forced to sell your home, or have it foreclosed, and your down payment plus all the principal payments you have made to date could be lost.

"On the other hand, if you are renting, it is much easier to downsize to a home you can afford. You have not invested any money in a down payment, so you don't have that money 'at risk'."

Joe, trying to capture this new view of renting, asked: "Does this mean I should not be trying to buy a house? I thought this whole session was about saving in the Home Fund?"

"The fact is that many young people should not worry about buying a home right away. We began this discussion with James expressing incredulity that he might wait 12 years before buying a home. I want you to feel comfortable waiting that long. There are lots of reasons that people should not buy homes, because if their lives are not settled, they will not be able to stay in one home long enough to make buying it a good investment."

The instructor stood up and went to the flip chart. "Think of life situations that could force you to need to move." As people shouted out there ideas, he copied them down:

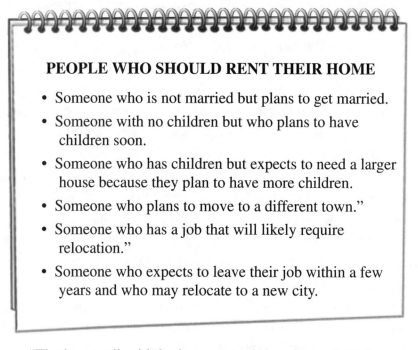

PEOPLE WHO SHOULD RENT THEIR HOME

- Someone who is not married but plans to get married.
- Someone with no children but who plans to have children soon.
- Someone who has children but expects to need a larger house because they plan to have more children.
- Someone who plans to move to a different town."
- Someone who has a job that will likely require relocation."
- Someone who expects to leave their job within a few years and who may relocate to a new city.

"That's great," said the instructor, sitting down. "All those are excellent reasons for someone to defer buying a house. People in these situations could contribute to their Home Fund, so that when their life circumstances change, they have the money saved to buy a home. But during the unsettled period, they should not feel that they are harming themselves financially by not owning a home. Instead, they should feel fortunate that they can take advantage of the low cost of renting to reduce their Housing Expense and increase their Annual Savings."

"I think I understand all this," said one woman, "but I still don't think I'd prefer to rent. It's not so easy to find a house for rent in the neighborhood I live in. I also like the control I have in owning my home. I don't want a landlord telling me what I can and cannot do to my home."

The instructor nodded sympathetically. "I don't mean to say you shouldn't buy a home if you want to. Conventional wisdom says that buying a home is financially advantageous. I want you all to know that for people who can't remain in their home long enough, the conventional wisdom is wrong. If you are one of those people, you can certainly choose to buy a home anyway, but you should recognize that if you move soon after you buy it, you'll have spent more than you would have by renting. You must balance the lifestyle benefits of owning your own home against the financial costs."

Sally listened to the discussion with great interest. Concern about her home had been a critical factor in her decision to attend the seminar. She hoped to find a solution that would enable her to move to a larger home. "What do we do now?" she asked.

"You have a couple of choices," answered the instructor. "First, if you can endure staying in your current home for a while longer, you help yourself the most in the long run. Concentrate for now on repaying debt and buying your all cash autos. After that, begin using your Annual Savings to prepay your mortgage. Here is the key: you only want to move one more time until you retire. Your next house should be the one that you and your children live in for most of your lives. The longer you stay in your current house, the greater your ability to build up equity in it, the more you will be able to afford the house you really want down the road.

"Ugh," said Sally. "I get it, but I don't like it. I just can't see staying here for another seven or eight years. What are the other choices?"

"The other choice," answered the instructor, "would be to sell your house now, assuming you can sell it for enough to at least repay your mortgage. Then, instead of buying another house now, you could rent. You could probably find an acceptable house to rent for less money than you are currently paying to own the house you live in now. Remember, renting normally requires a much lower annual cash expenditure than owning. Not only will you have a more acceptable home, you will lower your Housing Expense and increase your Annual Savings. You will pay off your debt quicker and then can begin to build up a Home Fund. It still could take seven or eight years before you move to your 'permanent home', but you may have a better living situation along the way."

Eric and Sally shared a glance of acceptance. Neither alternative excited them. They were not magic solutions. They were, however, viable solutions.

"I guess we never should have bought this house in the first place," Sally said.

"Unfortunately, you probably should not have," agreed the instructor. He turned to the flip chart and wrote:

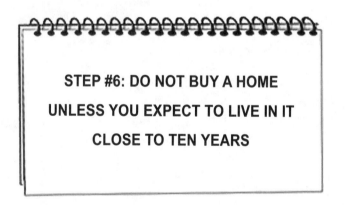

STEP #6: DO NOT BUY A HOME
UNLESS YOU EXPECT TO LIVE IN IT
CLOSE TO TEN YEARS

"Sally and Eric's dilemma shows the importance of step #6. Until you are confident you can live in a home close to ten years, you are better off renting. You should think of your lifetime home ownership in terms of three homes: a 'starter' home that you can live in for close to ten years, while you accumulate wealth for a larger home; a 'primary' home which you will live in most of your adult lives, and a 'retirement' home, often smaller than the primary home, where you will live when you have retired.

"What if you don't want to move to a retirement home? Can you just stay in the primary home?"

"Sure. It is fine to skip any of those homes. You could rent until you are 45 years old, and then buy a primary home. Or you could stay in your primary home forever, rather than moving to a retirement home. On the other hand, you don't want to add a fourth home to the list. Don't, as Sally and Eric did, plan to squeeze in a middle home between the starter home and the primary home. That's how you begin to destroy your wealth by moving too soon."

The instructor looked at his watch. The class had gone on ten minutes beyond schedule. Housing was such an important subject, and they had so much material to cover. They could have gone on and on. "We need to quit for today. Next week, we'll begin our discussion of investing."

Invest Wisely

CHAPTER SEVEN

Avoiding Risk

As Joe entered the classroom for the third session, he noticed that the participants had this time congregated into a single cluster. It appeared as if they had begun the discussion without waiting for the instructor. Jack and Isabel, a couple in their late-thirties, who Joe remembered having been relatively quiet in the first two sessions, dominated the conversation. Jack was narrating their unfortunate investing history as Joe edged into the crowd.

"When we got married in 1998, we received some money as a gift, so we invested it in the stock market," Jack recounted. "In those days, remember, everything was going up, but the internet stocks were really taking off. Experts romanticized the 'new economy', and we counted ourselves lucky to get in on the ground floor. I think we doubled our money in 1999. Well, you can guess what happened. When the market crashed in 2000, we lost close to 90%."

Isabel added to their tale: "Lots of the stocks we owned totally disappeared. These companies were worth billions of dollars one day, and the next day they were out of business. We couldn't believe it."

Jack interrupted her, "Most of them didn't go out of business, though, their stock price just kept falling and falling. At first, we thought, 'we'll just wait, we're in this for the long run, and eventually the prices will go back up'."

"Not only that," added Isabel, "we saw it as a 'buying opportunity', so we put as much of our savings into these internet stocks as we could while they were falling. And then they just kept falling."

"Eventually, we gave up," lamented Jack. "I don't know exactly when it was, 2002 or 2003, we just sold all our internet stocks and switched into blue chips. But by that time our portfolio had lost 90% of its value. All the money we'd saved was mostly gone, not to mention the wedding cash."

"Have you done better since?" asked Mitchell, a man in his fifties who was among the many people sympathetically listening to their story.

"Not really. A bit, maybe. We had a pretty good run for about five years, until 2008. We thought we'd learned our lesson about putting all our eggs in one basket, like when we only owned internet stocks. So we owned lots of different stocks in all areas. Big companies, small companies, growth stocks, value stocks, even some foreign stocks. We were saving money, and each month we'd buy a few more shares. Between our savings and the growth in our stocks, we even passed up the high point we'd hit in 2000."

"We had a little celebration," said Isabel ironically.

"Then, as you all know, at the end of 2008 everything went down. The big stocks, the little stocks, the foreign stocks, they all fell. We lost half our value in about six months. This time we said, 'we're not letting this happen again,' and we sold everything. Losing half was awful, but there was no way we were going to let ourselves lose 90%."

"What are you invested in now?"

"All cash," answered Isabel. "We know that is terrible, because our money won't grow, and we have barely more cash now than we had when we got married. But we are too scared to put it back in the stock market. We recognize we need to do something with our money, but we are feeling a little paralyzed right now."

Unobserved by Jack, Isabel, Joe, and most of the others, the instructor had edged into the circle and heard at least the latter part of Jack and Isabel's story. Numerous heads turned in surprise toward his voice as he commented: "You know Isabel, you have given me a wonderful lead-in to today's discussion. Sit down, everyone, and let's get started."

The instructor continued talking as people took their seats. "I suspect Jack and Isabel's story is similar to many or your investing experiences. Today's session will introduce Investing. Until now, we have focused on Saving: spending less than your net income, and utilizing your savings to pay off debt or to contribute to an Auto Fund or a Home Fund. We have been silent, so far, about how to invest the money in your Auto Fund and Home Fund. We will address that question today.

"I want to begin the discussion with the concept of risk. Unfortunately, the word risk has a variety of meanings, and we can't have a constructive discussion unless we all use the same definition. Let's begin with some of you telling us what risk means to you in the context of Investing. Any volunteers?"

Mitchell raised his hand. "I can tell you what I mean by risk. I don't like it. I'm pretty risk averse. I don't have a lot of money, and I can't afford to lose what I've got, so I try to avoid taking risk with my investments."

Andrea seemed to agree. "Isn't risk about taking chances? That's what 'taking a risk' means, right? I try to limit my risk by not taking chances."

Joe looked ready to disagree. "Sometimes you want to take risk, don't you? You can't earn the highest rates of return on your investments without taking some risk. There is a link between risk and return. The more risk you are willing to take, the higher return you expect to get."

Mark piped up in support of Joe. "I agree. You can't just say you want no risk. Sometimes I intentionally pick higher risk investments because that's how you make real money. I don't ignore risk, but I don't try to avoid it, either. I look at how risky each stock is before I buy it."

"How do you know how risky it is?" asked Andrea. "In my experience, some investments that seemed safe turned out to be surprisingly risky."

"I look at a stock's standard deviation and its beta," Mark responded. "The standard deviation tells me how much its return fluctuates, and the beta tells me how much its moves are linked to the overall stock market."

That answer didn't appear to satisfy Andrea at all. Another man, who had not been heard from during the first two sessions, seemed eager to add his own take on the subject. After introducing himself as Bruce, he expounded, "Look, isn't risk something that has been studied and analyzed in great detail by the finance community? I wouldn't call myself an expert in this area, but I've read enough to know that there is an industry full of people making a living analyzing the risk of all kinds of different stocks. I subscribe to some websites and newsletters which publish a bunch of different risk scores for each stock, including standard deviation and beta, but others as well."

A number of participants turned toward the instructor, unsure what Mark and Bruce were talking about. The instructor took the opportunity to guide the discussion in a different direction, "Mark and Bruce, you are getting a little technical. I am not looking for an academic definition of risk. I want to know what risk means to each of you. Let's return to Mitchell's first comment, which was, I think, that he didn't want to lose the money he has. Mitchell, is that right?"

"Yes, that's right," answered Mitchell. "I don't want to lose any money."

"Why not?"

Mitchell looked perplexed. "What do you mean, 'why not'?"

"Why not? Why don't you want to lose any money?"

"I need the money to pay for my kids' college tuition."

"Now we are getting somewhere," said the instructor. "Andrea, you also seemed reluctant to take risk. Are you afraid to lose money, too?"

"Sure."

"And why are you afraid to lose money? What do you need the money for?"

"I need it to pay my bills, for one thing."

"Okay, but we are discussing money you invest. What do you need that money for?"

Joe sees where the dialogue is leading. "You mean the money in our Home Fund and our Auto Fund, right? Losing money in those funds prevents us from buying the home or the car that we want."

"Exactly!" called the instructor. "If you have money invested in your Auto Fund, and the value of those investments falls, what is at risk? Your ability to buy the car. Here is a very simple and intuitive definition of risk." He walked over to the flip chart, and wrote:

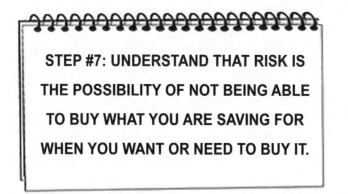

STEP #7: UNDERSTAND THAT RISK IS THE POSSIBILITY OF NOT BEING ABLE TO BUY WHAT YOU ARE SAVING FOR WHEN YOU WANT OR NEED TO BUY IT.

"Does this definition make sense to everybody?" asked the instructor as he returned to his seat.

Mitchell needed a little clarification. "So avoiding risk is just increasing the chances that you'll be able to buy what you want?"

"Yes, that's a good way to put it," replied the instructor.

"I'm not sure that works for me," Bruce said thoughtfully. "I think of risk in terms of a specific investment. Like I said before, many techniques can measure the risk of a particular investment. But I don't see how to tie an investment's risk to something external to the investment, like buying a car."

"Very insightful point, Bruce," said the instructor. "Do you all understand what Bruce is saying? Like Bruce, many of us are used to thinking about the risk of an investment without linking the investment to the eventual use of the money invested. That's a suitable mindset for a finance professor, but it doesn't help you much. To manage your investments effectively, you must ignore the more academic and technical definitions of risk and focus on what matters to you, which is your ability to achieve your personal financial objectives.

"This new mindset is amazingly simple. I'll demonstrate by using one of you as an example. Is there anyone in the class who has begun an Auto Fund yet? I know that most of your are in the debt repayment stage, but is there anyone lucky enough to be ready to have an Auto Fund?"

Jack raised his hand. Despite their travails in the stock market, he and Isabel were conscientious savers who had never run up any debt.

"Jack, tell us about your Auto Fund. How long before you expect to buy your car, and how much do you plan to spend?"

"Using the method you taught us last week, Isabel and I figured we could buy a car in about two years. The car we want costs about $20,000."

"Perfect." Speaking to everyone, the instructor continued, "Jack and Isabel should measure the riskiness of the investments they use in the Auto Fund by the likelihood that they will able to buy the car they have their eyes on in two years. The higher the likelihood, the lower the risk."

The body language in the class betrayed general confusion. "This is an abstract concept. I will make it more concrete. If you don't fully grasp my meaning yet, don't worry. You will understand better as we work through today's discussion. Let's continue with Jack and Isabel's Auto Fund example. Remember, they plan to buy a $20,000 car in two years. Can anyone think of the potential pitfalls that could prevent them from achieving that objective?"

"Their investments could go down," called Mitchell.

"Right," said the instructor. "As we've heard from Jack and Isabel, that has unfortunately been a recurring problem for them. What else? Suppose their investments do as well as they hope. Why else might they fail to achieve their objective?"

"They might not follow through on their savings plan," offered Eric.

"Another common pitfall," said the instructor. "Jack and Isabel appear to be very good savers, but unforeseen things can happen. If, for whatever reason, Jack and Isabel do not contribute to their Auto Fund at the rate they have planned, they will not achieve their objective. What else? There is one more pitfall lurking out there."

The class sat silently for a few moments, trying to identify the last pitfall. The instructor gave them a hint: "Since they have contributed as much as planned, and since the investments have performed as hoped, they will have about $20,000 in the Auto Fund in two years. If that is true, and they can't buy the car they are targeting, what must have happened?"

"The price of the car must have gone up," said Jack.

"Right. We ignored inflation. We'll deal with inflation more directly later today. For now, we need to recognize that significant inflation could jeopardize Jack and Isabel's ability to buy their car in two years."

He turned again to the flip chart and wrote:

THREE SOURCES OF RISK

1. Investment Risk

2. Behaviorial Risk

3. Inflation Risk

"Let's summarize the three sources of risk we have discussed. The first one is Investment Risk. So far we've focused most of our attention on Investment Risk. Investment Risk represents the possibility that our investments will perform below our expectations.

"The second risk, Behavioral Risk, represents the possibility that we might not follow through on our plan. We might contribute less than anticipated. Also, we might not invest the money as originally planned. Erratically switching investment strategies is a behavioral risk we will discuss further.

"The third risk, Inflation Risk, represents the possibility that the purchasing power of our money at the target date will not be sufficient to make the planned purchase."

The instructor paused to give everyone a chance to reflect on this framework. He wanted them to grasp the big picture. "Look," he said, "you all have come to this seminar to learn how to achieve your financial objectives. By minimizing risk, you increase the certainty that you will achieve your objectives. Minimizing risk requires addressing each type of risk, Investment Risk, Behavioral Risk, and Inflation Risk."

Bruce, who still conceived of risk as a function of a particular security, was not ready to accept this framework. "How much certainty can you really expect? Chasing certainty in investing is chasing a mirage. There are no sure things. That's the fun of it, though. It's like gambling. You take risks to have a chance at a big payoff."

When Bruce mentioned gambling, the instructor smiled. He jumped at the opportunity to distinguish Investing from gambling.

"Do you like to gamble, Bruce?" he asked.

"Sure, I love gambling. I love the action."

"Would gambling be as much fun if you knew, when you sat down at the table, exactly how much money you were going to win or lose?"

"No, that would ruin it," answered Bruce reluctantly.

"Of course it would. The excitement depends on not knowing whether you will win or lose. The fun of gambling depends upon uncertainty. Effective investing minimizes uncertainty. Gambling may be thrilling, but investing should not be."

"I still don't buy it," said Bruce. "I like the thrill of investing."

"If you find investing thrilling, you probably are focused on the big payoff, and not on your real objectives. It may be thrilling to wonder if you will strike it rich, but it is not thrilling to wonder if you will be able to buy the house you want. When you begin to think of investing in terms of achieving your real objectives, you will no longer find investing exciting. And that is a good thing."

"Why is that a good thing?" asked Mark. "I understand that we want more certainty and less risk, but I'm not sure I see why investing should be dull."

"What do all of you think? What is the advantage to making investing less exciting?"

For a moment no one said anything, then Isabel ventured an idea. "I suppose that if investing were less exciting, we could be less emotional and more rational. We might make better decisions."

"Good. What else?"

Eric explained, "If we're less emotional, we will more likely follow through on our plans. Speaking from experience, I find that I'll buy a stock that I am excited about, that I think has great long term prospects, and I plan to hold it for years. But if it is down after six months, I start to think I must have made a mistake, and I tend to get mad at myself for being stupid enough to buy that stock, so I end up selling it. I guess if I could be less emotional about the process I'd follow through on my original plan better."

"Do you all see what Eric is saying?" interjected the instructor. "He is talking about Behavioral Risk. Good, successful financial management is within our control. We just tend to mess it up. By better managing ourselves, we can dramatically change our outcomes. We can improve by extracting the excitement from investment process and focusing on our objectives."

"This will be a very new way of thinking for most of you. Remember Bruce's comment about thinking of risk in terms of a particular investment rather than something 'external' to it? We all have been taught to look at the 'risk' of a particular security in isolation. Changing that mindset takes work. Let's take a break now. When we return, we will discuss how to choose the investments in each fund in order to minimize the risk that you fail to achieve your objectives.

CHAPTER EIGHT

Investing Short-Term Funds

A s everybody returned after the break, an air of excitement pervaded the room. People's minds remained focused on the novel idea of thinking of risk in conjunction with achieving their goals. While they related to that concept on a gut level, they wondered how it would impact actual investment decisions.

The instructor began the discussion with a question: "What is the first question you need to ask yourself when you assess how to invest your money?"

A few people raised their hands with ideas. "The rate of return you are looking for," suggested one person.

"That's an important consideration, but it's not the starting point," said the instructor. "You need to think about something before you consider expected rates of return."

"The riskiness of each investment," suggested another.

"Minimizing risk is *what* we are trying to do," answered the instructor. "It's time to think about *how* to do it. Remember our definition of risk. What did we say that risk must be assessed in relation to?"

"The spending objective that you have," said Joe, who had been paying very close attention the whole time, though he'd said little this week.

"Right. And your spending objective has two components. How much you need to spend, and ..."

"When you need to spend it," said Joe, finishing the sentence.

"When you need to spend it," repeated the instructor. "The amount of time between when you make the investment and when you need to spend your money is called your Time Horizon. The first question to ask yourself when assessing how to invest your money is 'What is my Time Horizon?' Once you have answered that question, many other decisions easily fall into place."

"Can you explain what you mean by Time Horizon?" asked one man. "I'm not sure I understand."

"Remember our discussion a few minutes ago about Jack and Isabel's Auto Fund? They determined they could buy a $20,000 car about two years after they began to make contributions to the Auto Fund. In that case, their Time Horizon is two years at the date when they begins making contributions. Of course, after six months, their Time Horizon will have shrunk to eighteen months. The Time Horizon for your Funds will always be the length of time between the date the money is contributed and the date it will be spent. Does everyone understand?"

"I think so," said the man. "But why is that the first question you have to ask yourself?"

"Because," answered the instructor, "you can't evaluate the riskiness of any potential investment without knowing your Time Horizon. Certain types of investments, which are relatively low risk for short Time Horizons, are relatively higher risk for long Time Horizons, and vice versa. For example, fixed income investments are lower risk for short Time Horizons and higher risk for long Time Horizons, while equity investments are higher risk for short Time Horizons and lower risk for long Time Horizons."

Joe felt familiar with this distinction between equity and fixed income investments. Like most people, he had repeatedly heard advice recommending a long-term buy and hold strategy for equities, emphasizing that they will eventually pay off handsomely, even if you must endure some dips along the way. "I've been told that you want to own mostly stocks when you are younger, and then as you get older you shift more to fixed income investments. Is that what you are saying?" he asked.

"That is a bit of a misconception," said the instructor, "but like most misconceptions, it has a kernel of truth at the center of it. Time Horizon and age are not equivalent. Let's discuss this concept -- how many of you believe, or until this moment believed, that your appropriate mix of investments depends upon your age?"

Most hands went up. One man, in his sixties, spoke first: "I invested in one of those funds that automatically adjust your investments based upon your age. I'm 63 now, and I think it has me in 70% fixed income and 30% equities. It has been ratcheting down the equities slowly for some time now. I invested in it a number of years ago because I thought, 'That's great, it does all the work for me, and keeps me correctly invested.' Are you saying that isn't the right ratio for me?"

Joe followed him up. "I'm in 100% equities, because I thought that when you're my age, you should invest in stocks. I've got enough time to ride out the drops in the market."

The instructor held up his hands. "Look, everyone, Time Horizon and age are closely related when you are investing your Retirement Funds. Joe won't need his retirement funds for a very long time. He can endure a bumpy stock market. Similarly, people in their sixties should own a blend of equities and fixed income in their retirement accounts. We aren't ready to decide whether 30/70 is the correct ratio; other factors besides age do matter. When we discuss retirement investing in two weeks, we'll cover how to determine the correct ratio.

"Does the close relationship between age and Time Horizon persist when investing other Funds? Everyone, should Jack and Isabel consider their age when investing the money in their Auto Fund? Should they invest their Auto Fund differently than Joe or Andrea or Bruce or Mitchell should?"

This seemed like another trick question. Joe, who enjoyed them, took a shot: "I think their age must be important. I guess because they have more time to recoup losses than someone in their fifties or older."

"Does that sound right to all of you?" asked the instructor? "Can Jack and Isabel really better afford losses in their Auto Fund?"

"I don't think so," said Andrea. "You said the Time Horizon was the amount of time between when money is contributed to the Fund and when it is spent. Using that definition, age wouldn't matter for the Auto Fund, because it wouldn't affect how long before the money is spent."

"That's right, Andrea. The correspondence of age and asset allocation only applies to Retirement Funds! Don't extrapolate this correspondence to your other Funds. Look, we have spent a lot of time discussing how all of you should not invest in your Retirement Fund at all until you have paid cash for your car and probably bought your first house. The sooner Jack and Isabel buy their car, the sooner they can focus on long-term objectives. If they continue to lose money on their investments, they could have to wait a lot longer than two years to buy their car, pushing back everything else, too.

"Instead of thinking about your age, estimate the Time Horizon for the Fund whose money you will invest. Let's do the math so you can see how this works. Jack and Isabel have estimated that they can purchase a $20,000 car in two years. They will make equal contributions to their Auto Fund over the next 24 months, so their planned contribution must be about $833 per month.

"This simple estimation ignores our three risks: investment risk, behavioral risk, and inflation risk. Let's now take them into account so that we can determine the investment that minimizes the risk that Jack and Isabel fail to achieve their objective. Work backward and start with inflation risk. Assume inflation is 3% over the next two years. In the last thirty years, 3% is about average for inflation. Also assume they will stick with their plan, so we can continue to ignore behavioral risk. Jack, you told us that you've got all your money in cash now, right?"

"That's right. We just got too scared to stay in stocks."

"Okay, our final assumption will be that they keep their money in a FDIC insured checking account, earning no interest. Meanwhile, inflation will raise the price of the car they want. They will have to wait, therefore, about 25 ½ months instead of 24 months to buy their car.

"Another month and a half is not a big deal," said Isabel. "Is that really all?"

"Yes, a month and a half is the expected impact of inflation. You could invest a little more aggressively, using money market funds, bank CDs, Treasuries, or something that would at least keep up with inflation. If you do that, you still would need 25 months."

"If the investment keeps up with inflation, why can't they buy the car at 24 months, like they could without inflation?" asked one man.

"Good question," said the instructor. "Everyone pay attention – this detail is important. The price of the car increases at the rate of inflation over the entire two years. The investments, on the other hand, can only increase after Jack and Isabel contribute the money. Jack and Isabel will contribute the money equally over the two year Time Horizon. Those contributions made later have less time to grow. The contribution made in the first month will have 24 months to accumulate interest. The contribution made after 6 months will have only 18 months to accumulate interest. The final contribution will not have any time at all to accumulate interest.

"This dynamic has a significant impact. For short Time Horizons, the rate of return makes little difference unless it is badly negative. Even if Jack and Isabel invested their money in equities, and they perform well, earning their historical average of 9.5% per year, they would still need 23 ½ months to buy the car. A stock market return of 9.5% only accelerates their car purchase by two months compared to an FDIC guaranteed, no interest checking account!"

The instructor paused to give everyone a chance to catch up with him. He had made one of the most critical arguments of the session, and he wanted to make sure no one missed it.

"If that's true," said Jack, "we have nothing to gain by getting back into the stock market."

"Right," said the instructor, "but you have a lot to lose. Suppose the stock market falls at an annualized rate of 20% during this period. Instead of waiting 25 months, they will need 33 months. While, compared to a zero rate of return, normal equity returns only accelerate their purchase by two months, poor equity returns could delay their purchase much longer. I want you all to remember this example. It demonstrates extremely powerfully that you minimize risk for short Time Horizons by avoiding equities."

LET'S DO THE MATH

Auto Fund Dollar Goal	$20,000
Time Horizon (months)	24
Monthly contribution	$833.33
Assumed Inflation Rate	3%
Inflation adjusted Dollar Goal	$21,218
Months to achieve goal if Investing with a zero rate of return	25.5
Months to achieve goal if Investing with a 9.5% rate of return	23.5
Months to achieve goal if Investing with a -20% rate of return	33

"I understand your example," said one woman. "But what should you do if you can't wait two years to buy the car? Suppose your current car won't make it two more years. Shouldn't you invest more aggressively so that you might be able to buy the car sooner, even if only by a couple months?"

The instructor glanced around the group. "Does anyone remember a question similar to this from last week?"

James did: "Yes, we discussed the same question about my house. I could buy a $100,000 house in five years or a $140,000 house in seven years. We didn't discuss an option to accelerate the purchase by investing differently."

"No, we didn't," agreed the instructor. "We noted a trade-off between the purchase price and the savings time required. We weren't ready to discuss investing yet. Now I want everyone to take another look at both problems. You can see that the issue is the same. Do you think a more aggressive investment would be the right choice if you want to buy the car or the house sooner?"

Joe felt confident he knew the answer. "I think, at least for Jack and Isabel's car, buying stocks makes no sense. To buy the car two months sooner, they would need to take a big risk. If they can't wait two years, they should either buy a less expensive car or save more money each month."

The instructor turned to the woman. "Do you see Joe's point? You may need to replace your car in less than two years. But given such a short Time Horizon, you cannot hope to use an investing strategy to accelerate your purchase. You can only do it the two ways Joe suggested: increasing your monthly contribution to the Auto Fund or settling for a less expensive car."

"Is it different for me and my house?" asked James. "For me to buy the $140,000 house, it would take seven years of contributing to the Home Fund. Can I invest the money in my Home Fund more aggressively to reduce that time?"

"I'd like everyone's opinion on that," answered the instructor. "Clearly, two years is not a long enough Time Horizon to invest in equities. What do you think is long enough? Five years? Seven years? Ten years? Twenty years? Who thinks that seven years is a long enough Time Horizon to invest in equities?"

Most of the class took some time to think about it, but a few hands rose immediately, and several more rose after a few seconds. Mark spoke for those who believed seven years is long enough: "Seven years seems like plenty of time. I know you can have some bad years, but if you stick with your stocks, I think most of the time you will come out ahead."

Bruce agreed, for a slightly different reason. "I would worry about inflation over a seven year period. If you have your money in a checking account for seven years, inflation could kill you. That $140,000 house will cost a lot more in seven years. Inflation might not be a very big deal for two years but over seven years it will definitely matter."

Mitchell disagreed. "What you're saying about inflation makes sense, but I'd be afraid to invest in stocks if my Time Horizon is seven years. Look at the last seven years in the market. It's been awful. I know my stocks are worth a lot less now than they were seven years ago."

"I agree," piped in Sally. "When you talk about risk, to me, stocks are the embodiment of risk. They go up, they go down – you never know what they're going to be worth. I can't envision putting the money I'm saving to buy a house into stocks."

Everyone seemed to make sense. Who was right? The group looked to the instructor for some clarity. "This is a tricky question," he told them. "First, let's do a little more math, so you can see more concretely what the issues are. Then we'll try to draw some conclusions.

The instructor turned to the flip chart and began writing as he talked. "James plans to buy a house that costs $140,000, and our rule of thumb says he will need seven years. But Bruce's point is very true: inflation matters more over seven years than over two. If Inflation Risk averages 3% a year for seven years, by the time James has enough money in his Home Fund to make the down payment, the house will cost $172,182."

"You're assuming inflation will be three percent," added Bruce. "It could turn out to be much higher."

"That's also true. Inflation is fairly easy to predict for the next two years. Over seven years, however, it could change unexpectedly. We need to remember that as we consider this example. Still, for now let's keep inflation at 3%, as that's our best guess.

"If James puts the money in his Home Fund into a no-interest checking account, the effect of inflation will force him to wait 104 months instead of 84 months. That's almost two extra years. By choosing fixed income investments that match inflation, he can reduce his wait time by almost a year, cutting it to 94 months. Still, he must wait an extra 10 months to buy his house because of inflation. Of course, that's just an estimate; if inflation were higher or lower than three percent, his wait time would change.

"If James instead invests in stocks and achieves the historical average return of 9.5%, he could buy his house much sooner. He could buy the house in 75 months, 19 months less than the wait time required for an investment strategy that simply matched inflation."

"I think 19 months is enough to matter," said James. I understand that two months doesn't matter for the auto fund. That makes sense to me. But if I have to wait an extra 19 months to buy a house if I don't invest in equities, I think equities are worth the risk."

"Wait a minute. We haven't seen the risk yet," answered Andrea. Aren't you going to show us how long he'd have to wait to buy his house if the stocks go down?" she asked the instructor.

"I sure am. For this example, suppose the stocks go down an average of 2% per year. That may not seem like a lot, but two percent losses per year for seven or more years is a very bad outcome for stocks. Consistently bad stock returns for that long are relatively rare. But it can happen, and if it does, you are stuck. You now have to wait 128 months to buy your house. That's about three years longer than you would have had to wait if you'd stuck with the fixed income strategy that gets you the house in 94 months."

"That's what I've been saying!" exclaimed Mitchell. "I don't know about the rest of you, but I don't like that risk. If it were me, I could never have held the stocks that long, anyway. I'd have sold them when they started going down."

"Did you all hear what Mitchell said? That he would have sold the stocks when they went down?" asked the instructor. "Hold that thought - I want to come back to that in just a minute. First, let's summarize a bit. The difference between a stock portfolio and a fixed income portfolio is likely to be about 19 months, if your starting Time Horizon was 7 years. That seems like a big enough difference that you'd want to invest in stocks.

"On the other hand, if you catch a bad stretch in the stock market, instead of buying the house in 6 1/4 years, as you had estimated you would, you could have to wait 10 ½ years. You have a great deal of uncertainty regarding how long it will take you to buy your house. However, if you go the fixed income route, you can rest comfortably knowing that you will be able to buy your house in about 8 years, maybe a few months less.

LET'S DO THE MATH

Home Fund Dollar Goal	$35,000
(25% of $140,000)	
Time Horizon (months)	84
Monthly contribution	$416.67
Assumed Inflation Rate	3%
Inflation adjusted Dollar Goal	$43,046
Months to achieve goal if Investing with a zero rate of return	104
Months to achieve goal if Investing with a 3% rate of return	94
Months to achieve goal if Investing with a 9.5% rate of return	75
Months to achieve goal if Investing with a -2% rate of return	128

"Let's pause for a minute and take a little poll. Which of you feel the shorter expected time to buy the house is worth the extra uncertainty, and which of you prefer the reliability of knowing more precisely how long you need?"

The hands were about equally split. The participants looked around the room and saw no clear consensus. "So," asked one woman, "does that mean at seven years, your investment strategy depends on your personal preferences?"

"No," said the instructor, "there is another wrinkle we need to consider. The problem with the analysis as I've presented it is that the stock market does not move smoothly. At any point in time, stock values could fall precipitously. Suppose James invests his Home Fund in stocks for five years, and the value grows as expected. He now needs a little more than a year to reach his goal. Does it make sense for him to remain invested in stocks at that point, knowing that he could suddenly lose 20% or more of the money in his Home Fund? It does not. In fact, his situation now looks quite similar to the situation we saw with Jack and Isabel's Auto Fund. With a remaining Time Horizon of two years or less, equities don't belong in the Fund."

"If that is true," pondered Joe, "doesn't that change your initial Time Horizon?" You don't have a seven year Time Horizon if you must sell your equities after five years, right? You have a five year Time Horizon."

While some members of the class struggled to comprehend Joe's point, Andrea was a step ahead. She had sensed all along a flaw in this analysis, and Joe helped her pinpoint it. "If you think about it, Joe, you don't even have a five year Time Horizon. If you know you must sell your equities after five years, then after three years, you again only have two years left. That would imply you really have a three year Time Horizon. You could extend this logic back forever, and you'd never have a long enough Time Horizon to buy equities."

Andrea's comment confused some people. The concept of Time Horizon seemed simple when the instructor first presented it, but this discussion substantially complicated the idea.

"It is a bit of a paradox," commented the instructor. "And it's a valuable lesson. Theoretically, it might seem logical to invest your Home Fund or Auto Fund in equities if your Time Horizon is five to seven years. More often than not, that strategy will allow you to buy your home or car sooner. Unfortunately, that strategy has a major flaw. You can afford to invest in equities at the beginning, when you have a small amount of money invested, and the losses won't hurt you much. As the Time Horizon narrows, however, and the amount of money you have contributed to your Fund grows, you can no longer afford the risk of a dramatic drop in the value of your equities, so you are forced to shift to fixed income."

"So what is James' Time Horizon?" asked Joe. "Is it seven years, or is it less?"

"His Time Horizon is still seven years, at least in the beginning. The lesson is that a seven year Time Horizon is not long enough to invest in equities. Seven years does not allow you enough time to benefit from equity growth before you need to switch to fixed income investments.

He turned to the flip chart and wrote:

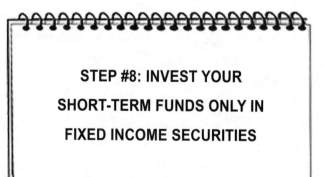

STEP #8: INVEST YOUR

SHORT-TERM FUNDS ONLY IN

FIXED INCOME SECURITIES

"Investing in equities for only the first couple years has only a modest impact on reducing the actual wait time. You only save a few months on a seven year Time Horizon. Even with a seven year Time Horizon, therefore, you should stick with an all fixed income investment strategy. Such a strategy is easy to follow and very predictable. You can accurately forecast, even well into the future, the date you will buy your home or car. While that time period might be a little longer than you might need using an all equity strategy, the trade-off is worth it."

"I see what you are saying," said Jack, "but I don't know that I agree that the trade-off is worth it. You keep telling us to avoid equities, but over our whole life, won't we forgo a huge amount of appreciation in value?"

"Listen to your question. 'Over your whole life' you would forgo a huge amount of value. If your Time Horizon is your whole life, invest in equities. At stake for James is not 'a huge amount of value', only the need to wait an extra year and a half to buy his home. As we discussed last week, waiting a little longer to buy your home is fine. He can still buy the home he wants. He will still have time to save for college and retirement. Plus, he can have extremely high confidence that his plan will succeed. Remember Mitchell's comment about selling his stocks when they were down. I want to discuss that comment now.

"We have glossed over Behavioral Risk so far. Unfortunately, Behavioral Risk is a huge problem. Bad investment decisions do tremendous damage. Part of the difficulties you and Isabel have had stem from unlucky timing in the stock market. But poor decision-making exacerbated your pain. You are far more likely to avoid bad decisions when investing your Auto and Home Fund if you stick to fixed income securities."

Jack was still not fully convinced. "I hear what you're saying, but it doesn't feel right to me. At my age, I feel like I should be investing in equities. According to what I'm learning here, I am supposed to invest first in an Auto Fund, and not use any equities. Then I'm supposed to contribute to a Home Fund, and not invest in any equities. Then, by the time I'm ready to save for anything else, I'll be too old to invest in equities, so I'll spend my whole life buying nothing but bonds!"

"Don't worry, you won't be," assured the instructor. Later today we'll begin talking about investing with longer Time Horizons. When we do, you'll see that we focus primarily on equities. With a long enough Time Horizon, equities have some big advantages. Their higher rate of return has plenty of time to compound, so the difference between investing in equities and investing in fixed income becomes extremely large. Also, equities have a consistent long-run track record. You can be more confident in predicting their performance in the long run than the short run.

"In the short run, those advantages reverse. The difference in growth between investing in equities and fixed income is minimal, and equities produce very inconsistent rates of return. That, in a nutshell, explains why you begin thinking about investing by knowing your Time Horizon.

"Let's take a break. Before we end our discussion of investing your short-term Funds, we need to evaluate the various fixed income investment vehicles you can choose for your Funds."

CHAPTER NINE

Choosing Fixed Income Securities

T he instructor scanned the room to gauge the students' moods as they re-entered the room after the break. He expected them to look a little deflated. Although advertisements for the seminar had not promised a get-rich-quick scheme, people naturally hope for secrets to easy success. The admonition to avoid stocks for their Home and Auto Funds, though people might understand the rationale, would likely generate some disappointment and resistance.

The instructor, however, also noticed some more upbeat feelings. These positive vibes appeared to emanate from a confidence level not apparent at either of the first two sessions. The confidence flowed from the knowledge growing among the participants, and the recognition that they could apply this knowledge to ultimately, if not quickly, achieve financial success.

The instructor said, "Let's review what we have covered today, in our class dedicated to Investing. We began by discussing risk, what risk means, and the different components of risk: Investment Risk, Behavioral Risk, and Inflation Risk. We defined risk as the possibility that we will not meet our financial objectives. We then determined that we can minimize risk for our short-term objectives by avoiding equities and utilizing fixed income securities. While we talked a little bit about fixed income securities, we didn't discuss how to select specific fixed income securities to buy. It's now time to circle back and fill that gap."

"First, let's be specific about what a fixed income security is. Can anyone give examples of fixed income securities? Just shout the types out and I'll write them down."

"Bonds."

"Treasury bills."

"Bank CDs."

"Commercial paper."

"Good," said the instructor when he'd finished writing them down. Can anyone tell me what all of those securities have in common? What is it about them that makes them 'fixed-income'?"

As a banker, Joe felt confident he knew the answer. "Fixed income securities are a loan from you to a borrower. You get paid a set amount of interest, plus you get your money back at some future date."

"Who is the borrower?" asked one woman.

"The borrower could be almost anyone. If you buy government bonds, the government is the borrower. If you buy corporate bonds, the company is the borrower. Or, if you put your money in a bank, the bank is the borrower."

"And I am the lender when I buy a bond or put money in the bank?" asked the woman uncertainly.

"That's exactly right," said the instructor, encouragingly. "It is useful to think of yourself as a lender, too. Consider the process we have discussed from the first session of this seminar as transforming you from a borrower into a lender. Instead of borrowing money from credit card companies, you will lend it to businesses and governments."

"I've put money in the bank, of course," said the woman, "but I'm not familiar with bonds or commercial paper or some of the other things on your list. How do I know which of those to buy?"

"Does it matter that much?" asked Bruce. Aren't we using fixed income investments because they are pretty much risk free?"

"No, they're not risk free at all," answered the instructor. "Don't get lulled into thinking that. While, for short Time Horizons, fixed income investments allow you to minimize risk, they don't eliminate risk. Let's discuss their risks. There are two primary sources of Investment Risk in fixed income securities, credit risk and interest rate risk."

He turned to the flip chart and wrote:

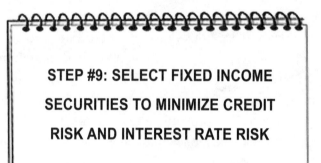

STEP #9: SELECT FIXED INCOME SECURITIES TO MINIMIZE CREDIT RISK AND INTEREST RATE RISK

"How do we do that?" asked Andrea.

"I'm going to show you," the instructor replied. "Start with Credit Risk. Can anyone explain what we mean by Credit Risk?"

"Sure," said Joe. "Credit Risk is the possibility that the borrower won't pay you back."

"Good," said the instructor. He turned to the class, "What do you all think? Are all borrowers equally likely to pay you back, or are some more creditworthy than others?"

A chorus agreed that some are more creditworthy than others. "Of course," said the instructor. "If you lend money to the U.S. Government by buying Treasury Bills, you have a near certainty of receiving your money when due. On the other hand, if you lend your cousin Charlie $50,000 to open a restaurant, you may never see that money again.

"In general, more creditworthy borrowers pay lower interest rates. To induce you to lend money to Cousin Charlie, he will have to pay you a high interest rate. On the other hand, the U.S. Government pays less interest than just about anyone else."

"Suppose you don't lend to the government and you don't lend to your Cousin Charlie. Instead, you choose something in between. Suppose you lend to a company, buying the bonds of, say, Wal-Mart. Assume those bonds have a maturity date of ten years from the date you buy them. You can hold the bonds for ten years and Wal-Mart will pay you interest payments each year, and at the end of ten years Wal-Mart will pay you the face value of the bonds.

If you bought these bonds for your Auto Fund, you may want sell them after two years. By then, you may have enough money in the fund to buy your car. Because the maturity date of the bond is eight years away, to obtain the cash to buy your car, you need to sell the Wal-Mart bonds. No problem, a ready market exists to buy the bonds from you. The question is, how much can you sell them for?"

"It depends," answered Joe. "If Wal-Mart has been successful, you might sell the bonds for more than you paid. But if they've been unsuccessful, you could receive a lot less."

"Why would you get less than you paid?" asked one woman.

"The bonds' value will fall if people fear Wal-Mart won't be able to pay its debts. Think about General Motors and Chrysler. Their bondholders lost billions when those companies filed for bankruptcy. If investors fear a potential bankruptcy, they won't want to buy the bonds, and their price will fall."

"I thought you said fixed income securities are low risk. If their prices can fall like that, why are they better than stocks?"

"Some of them are not," answered the instructor. "Don't succumb to the temptation to invest in high-yield bonds – what used to be called 'junk bonds' – in order to capture higher interest than bonds issued by more creditworthy borrowers pay. For the same reason you avoid equities in your Auto and Home Funds, you should avoid high-yield bonds."

"What if you use a mutual fund?" asked Mitchell. "Can't you avoid credit risk by buying a high-yield bond fund instead of buying individual bonds?"

"That's a great question. Before I answer it, let's make sure everyone understands what a mutual fund does. You can all buy shares of a mutual fund, which invests on your behalf. There are mutual funds that invest in almost any imaginable type of security. A high-yield bond fund may own the bonds of 100 or more companies. In theory, if one or two of them default on their bonds, the fund is barely affected."

"When you say 'in theory'," said Mitchell, "it makes me think there is an 'in practice' coming. What is the problem with mutual funds?"

"The problem isn't with mutual funds in general, it is with a mutual fund that buys high-yield bonds. Compared to buying individual high-yield bonds, you are better off buying a bond fund. But a mutual fund can't eliminate credit risk. During a recession, most companies which have issued high-yield bonds will suffer, and the prices of their bonds will fall. While few will actually default, the falling prices of the bonds will still cause the value of the mutual fund shares to fall. Your investment could lose money."

"But," said Bruce, "you just told us that these fixed income investments are not risk free. Is the possibility of losing money a good trade-off for the higher interest rate?"

"It's not. Gaining an extra couple percent interest by buying a high-yield bond fund instead of a fund made up of investment grade corporate bonds or government bonds is not a worthwhile trade. Remember, your short-term objectives don't benefit much from a higher rate of return. Investing the money in your Auto Fund into a high-yield bond fund instead of an investment grade bond fund might only accelerate the purchase of your car by a couple of weeks!"

"That makes sense," said Mitchell. "What should we buy, then?"

"There are a variety of fixed income securities you can buy which have almost negligible credit risk. The safest choice is anything backed by the U.S. Government. The U.S. Treasury sells a variety of securities of varying duration. It also sells a type of bond called TIPS, which has a rate of return that is tied to the inflation rate. You can easily buy these directly from the U.S. Treasury. Equally safe are deposits and savings in banks, up to the limit guaranteed by the FDIC.

"Nearly as safe are bonds issued by municipalities. Because municipalities do, on rare occasions, default on their debts, don't hold municipal bonds directly; hold them in a mutual fund. Municipal bonds have a big benefit: the federal government does not tax their interest.

"Finally, reasonably safe are investment grade corporate bonds if held in a mutual fund. During a severe recession or credit crisis those funds may lose some value, but not too much. The companies whose bonds these funds own rarely default. The slightly higher interest rate paid by these companies, in comparison to the interest rate paid by the U.S government, offers a reasonable trade-off for the slightly higher but still limited risk of a decline in value due to credit risk."

The instructor paused for a moment. He had presented a lot of material, and he worried about it being dry and technical. He couldn't avoid it. Even if the participants grasped the big picture concepts that he'd spent the beginning of the session discussing, they could do grievous damage by accidentally choosing the wrong investments. Making matters worse, he knew the most technically complex section remained.

Taking a deep breath, he continued: "So far we have focused on credit risk, one of the two types of risk inherent in fixed-income securities. The second type is interest rate risk. Changes in the global market for interest rates will increase or decrease the value of the fixed-income securities you own. A wide variety of factors affect that market, moving interest rates continually up and down. Such factors include forecasts of economic growth, forecasts of inflation, international currency exchange rates, changes in international trade, and policy decisions by central banks around the world."

"Do we need to remember all this?" asked one man.

"No, you sure don't. You need to remember that interest rates fluctuate, and the movement of interest rates changes the value of the bonds you own."

"Why do changing interest rates change the value of the bonds I own?"

"Let's do a little math and it will be clear. Suppose you buy a $100 Treasury bond, paying interest at 4%, and due in 30 years. You buy it for your Home Fund, which has a Time Horizon of five years. During the next five years you will receive two payments per year of $2 each, a total of $4 per year. That is your four percent interest. At the end of five years you will sell the note, and you expect to receive your $100 back at that time.

"The actual price you will receive in five years depends on the level of interest rates at that time. If interest rates on Treasury notes have risen from 4% to 6%, you will not receive $100, you will receive less. Does anyone know why?"

Joe responded, "Because the new notes issued by the Treasury will be paying $6 per year instead of $4 per year. Since your note only comes with payments of $4 per year, it is less desirable." Joe's banking knowledge was proving quite valuable in this session.

"That's exactly right. The price of your note must fall so that a buyer of the note will earn the same 6% interest rate that he would earn if he bought a fresh one directly from the U.S. Treasury. In this case, the price will fall to $74.27. When you sell the note after five years, instead of paying your $100 back, the buyer will pay only $74.27."

"Really? I thought these bonds were supposed to be so safe. Between the credit risk and now the interest rates, it seems these are very risky, too," Mitchell lamented.

"I agree," added Isabel. "You started today by convincing us we shouldn't invest in equities because they are too risky. Now you showed us we can lose money with bonds, too. So what should we do, put our money under the mattress?"

The questions heartened the instructor. He intended to demonstrate that bonds have risks, and he had succeeded. "You can't mindlessly buy fixed-income investments. We discussed credit risk, and how it can cause significant losses. But we also discussed how to eliminate virtually all of that risk by selecting the right type of fixed income securities. I will now show you how to eliminate virtually all interest rate risk, too.

"You can eliminate interest rate risk by owning bonds that mature at the right time. Your bonds should mature when you expect to spend the money on your savings objective. For example, if you estimate that you will have enough money in your Auto Fund to buy a car in July, 2013, you would want the bonds in your Auto Fund to mature as close as possible to July, 2013.

"In the example we just used, the $100 Treasury note sold for $74.27 because interest rates had risen in the five years since the note was purchased. The new buyer of the note would only pay $74.27 because they were entitled to receive 6% interest. If, however, the note were maturing, the U.S. Treasury would have paid the whole $100! If you hold your fixed income investments to maturity, you will always receive the full face value."

"That sounds good in theory," said Jack, "but, realistically, you can't be so accurate in estimating when you will buy your car or your house or whatever. You can't hit the date right on the nose so that your bonds all mature at exactly the right time."

"No, you're right, you can't," agreed the instructor. "But you don't need perfection. Suppose you bought a Treasury bill that matured in the month when you expected you'd be able to buy a house, which was five years in the future. Now, suppose you've saved a bit more than you thought you could, so you want to sell your Treasury bill and buy the house six months early. Will you still have to sell it for $74.27? What does everyone think?"

"I guess so, if interest rates still have risen from 4% to 6%," proposed one man.

"Interest rates have still risen, but something very important has changed. Who knows what it is?"

Joe answered, "The buyer of the Treasury note will only hold it for six months until it matures, instead of for twenty-five years. The lower interest rate has much less impact on him."

"Bingo," said the instructor. "The buyer of this Treasury note will pay $99.03, hardly any discount at all from $100. As long as your bonds mature close to the time you expect to need the money, changes in interest rates will not affect you much."

LET'S DO THE MATH

Face Value	$100
Annual Interest Payment	$4
Market Interest Rate when Purchased	4%
Years to Maturity	30
Cost to Purchase Bond	$100.00
Face Value	$100
Annual Interest Payment	$4
Market Interest Rate when Sold	6%
Years to Maturity	25
Amount Received When Selling Bond	**$74.27**
Face Value	$100
Annual Interest Payment	$4
Market Interest Rate when Sold	6%
Years to Maturity	0.5
Amount Received When Selling Bond	**$99.03**

"Isn't it hard to do this in practice?" asked Jack skeptically. "How do you make all your investments mature on the right date?"

"It's really quite simple," answered the instructor. "If you buy individual bonds, simply buy bonds with the right maturity date. You can buy Treasury bonds direct from the U.S. Treasury in increments of $100. If you are contributing $600 per month to your Auto Fund, each month you purchase six $100 bonds online, all with the same maturity date at www.Treasurydirect.com."

"What if you are saving $625 per month? What do you do with the extra $25."

"Just put it in a savings account. Every four months, you will have accumulated another $100, so every four months, instead of buying six $100 notes, you will buy seven."

"That makes sense if you use Treasuries," said Mark. "Treasuries don't work for me, because I'm in a high tax bracket. I'd prefer buying tax-free municipal bonds. You said not to buy them directly, to buy them in a mutual fund. Fine, but mutual funds don't have a maturity date. What do I do?"

"Excellent point, Mark. Mutual funds don't allow the same precision as treasuries provide. Therefore, if you choose the mutual fund route, you must endure slightly more interest rate risk, as you must endure slightly more credit risk. Still, you can manage the risk. Does anyone know how?"

"Don't mutual funds publish the average duration of their bonds?" suggested Joe.

"Yes, they do. Suppose a mutual fund has 100 bonds in its portfolio. Some mature in a few months, some in a year, some in two years, some in three or more years. The average maturity of those bonds is called the funds' 'duration'. Choose a mutual fund whose duration approximately matches your Time Horizon. If your Time Horizon is five years, any fund with a duration of three to six years would be an adequate choice."[4]

"What if the duration changes while you own the fund? The funds don't have to always keep it the same, do they?"

"No, the duration will fluctuate, at least somewhat. The manager of the mutual fund may change the duration to take advantage of opportunities to maximize the fund's rate of return. Still, each mutual fund normally operates within general guidelines. As you research fund alternatives, investigate their history of maintaining a consistent duration."

"I see another problem," said Mark. "If you own a bond, as your Time Horizon shrinks with the passage of time, the time to maturity for your bond shrinks equally. If you own a mutual fund, a gap will eventually open between your Time Horizon, which shrinks, and the fund's duration, which remains constant."

Mark's insight impressed the entire class, including the instructor. "You're right," he said. "To maintain a balance between your Time Horizon and your mutual funds' duration, you must periodically change funds if your initial Time Horizon was long enough. If you begin with a Time Horizon of five years or more, you'll want to move your money to a different fund with a shorter duration about half way to your goal."

---

4   Because you will hold the fund for at least a couple years, a duration slightly below your initial Time Horizon more closely matches the results of a bond held to maturity.

"This seems so complicated," said Isabel. "Should we avoid mutual funds because we can't pinpoint the maturity date as close as we can buying individual Treasuries?"

Isabel's question offered an opportunity for the instructor to transition back from the technical detail of the discussion to more universal advice. "No, you don't need to avoid mutual funds. I want to make a general comment. You don't need to seek perfection in your financial management. I want you to learn in this class how to make predominantly good decisions. As long as you make predominantly good decisions, you will prosper.

"A brief summary. Begin by making sure your spending is proportional to your net income. Use your savings to eliminate debt. Build on that foundation by saving money to buy a car and a house. Invest wisely by avoiding unnecessary risks. For your short-term Funds, avoid equities and high-yield bonds; instead, buy very creditworthy bonds of approximately the same duration as your Time Horizon. Don't buy 30-year bonds to sneak an extra couple percent of interest. Don't buy shares in a mutual fund that invests in very long duration bonds. At the same time, don't worry about the difference between a duration of three years and five years. It won't affect you much."

The students looked exhausted. The technical information had been hard for everyone to follow. "Look," said the instructor. "I'm trying to show you that, when all is said and done, you do not achieve your short-term objectives with great investing. Achieving your short-term objectives requires saving adequately and not investing poorly. You can invest in regular Treasuries or TIPS. You can buy mutual funds that invest in municipal bonds or investment grade corporate bonds. Whatever route you choose, don't expect to achieve your short-term objectives through aggressive investment growth. Let's take one final break today. Investment growth will be our subject when we return to discuss long-term investing strategies."

CHAPTER TEN

Investing in Equities

The instructor allowed everyone to take an extra long break. They needed the time to mentally rest after the intensity and complexity of the preceding discussion. In addition, he wanted them to feel like they were starting fresh. The concluding portion of the investing class marked an important transition. When everyone had returned, he began by highlighting the new phase they were about to begin: "Until now, our seminar has focused on short-term objectives. In an important sense, this moment marks the beginning of the second half of the seminar. From here on, we will focus on long-term objectives.

"When we discussed your Home and Auto Funds, we concluded that you should use fixed income investments. At that time, we alluded to the idea that equity investments would play a primary role in your long-term Funds. During the next two sessions, we'll discuss setting up and contributing to your College Fund and your Retirement Fund, the two main long-term Funds for most people. Today, while on the subject of investing, we will address two key questions about investing in equities: 1) what rate of return can you expect to earn, and 2) what securities should you invest in to achieve that return?

"Before diving into these questions, I'd like some of you to share your thoughts on investing in equities. We need to remind ourselves of the pitfalls of equity investing. It may seem like a while ago that Jack and Isabel began today's session with the sad tale of their experience investing in equities. Does anyone else have a story they'd be willing to share?"

Eric explained, "I've lost some money, too. I don't think of myself as a very aggressive investor, but I like to buy a stock when I feel like it's a good bargain. Every once in a while I look at a stock and think, 'that price doesn't make sense,' so I'll buy a few shares. Sometimes I'm right, but I'd have to say that more often than not I'm wrong, or at least I sell the stock too soon or too late. I think if I were better at timing my purchases and sales, I'd have made more money."

Eric's comment animated Mitchell, a man in his mid-fifties: "I just don't think you can get the timing right. It's almost impossible. Stocks move unpredictably, especially when they are going down. I'm not a fan of stock investing. I've seen too many people lose too much money," he said.

Mark was in the opposite camp and looked eager to share his perspective: "Sure, you can lose money in the stock market. I've lost plenty. But I've also made a lot of money, too. If you want to make money investing, you can't just stay away from stocks. We've been talking all day about how you earn very little with your fixed income investments. With my equity investments, I shoot for fifteen percent returns."

"You shoot for them, but do you get them?" countered Mitchell.

"Let's not get into one individual's results," interrupted the instructor, stopping the discussion before it veered off course. "I thought it was important that we all remind ourselves of the Investment Risk inherent in equity investing. The comments of Jack and Isabel, Eric, and Mitchell all served that purpose. But Mark's point is valid, too. Equity investing is our only real defense against

Inflation Risk. Over time, inflation normally erodes most of the gains from fixed income investing. If you want your investments to grow, you need to invest in equities."

"Until now, though, you've been telling us not to invest in equities," said Isabel, a little confused.

"Until now we've been discussing investing your short-term Funds, which have short Time Horizons. For short Time Horizons, investment growth doesn't matter much. You can forgo growth without materially impacting the length of time you must save to achieve your goals. For the rest of this seminar, we will discuss achieving your long-term objectives. For those objectives, you will have long investment Time Horizons, which allows investment growth to have a substantial impact on helping you achieve your goals. To benefit from that growth, you will need to invest in equities."

"So for our Auto Fund and our Home Fund, you still don't want us to invest in equities," said Isabel, confirming she understood.

"Right," said the instructor, "but for your College Fund and your Retirement Fund, which will be the subject of our next two sessions, most of you will want to invest in equities. Everyone understand?"

He surveyed the room. People seemed to recognize the distinction he had made, so he continued the discussion.

"The first question I said we would address regarding equity investing is 'what rate of return can you expect to earn'? Mark told us that he shoots for fifteen percent. What about the rest of you? What rate of return do you think you should earn on your equity investments? Give your answer in after-inflation, or constant, dollars."

"Twenty percent."

"No way, that's too high. Eight percent."

"Still too high. Six percent."

"Twelve percent."

"Fifteen percent."

"My number is negative. I usually lose money."

The instructor smiled at the divergence of opinion. Of all the subjects they had discussed, this one seemed to generate the broadest array of views: "Obviously, you have some differing opinions on this question. And yet, this is really a question of fact. There is very good historical data on the subject of stock market returns.

"Research has shown remarkable consistency in equity returns over the past 200 years. Looking back over that period, equities have earned an after-inflation rate of return between 6.5 and 7 percent for the entire period, as well as for most major sub-periods."

The instructor stood up and turned to the flip chart. He wrote the following:

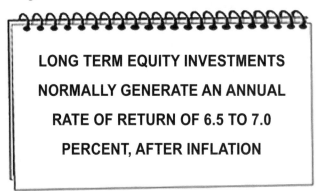

LONG TERM EQUITY INVESTMENTS
NORMALLY GENERATE AN ANNUAL
RATE OF RETURN OF 6.5 TO 7.0
PERCENT, AFTER INFLATION

Mitchell looked perplexed. "I don't know what you're talking about. There is nothing consistent about equities. They go up, they go down. Some years they're up 20%, the next year they're down 30%."

"Good point," said the instructor, "Let me clarify. Equities show no consistency over short periods. They do show surprising consistency over long periods. The longer your Time Horizon, the more confident you can be that your actual equity returns will come close to the historical average."

"Wait a second," said Andrea, "I don't see why the results from the 1800s have any bearing on what stocks will earn today. Think of the differences between the present and 200 years ago. If the world has changed, how can you say that today's stock returns will be the same as the historical average?"

Andrea had a way of capturing the general unease within the class and putting it into words. She kept the instructor on his toes. As usual, however, he had a ready answer: "It seems hard to believe, doesn't it? Think of all the changes: the introduction of technology, globalization of the economy and world markets. Back in the 1800s, nearly all the stocks were railroads and utilities. And yet, in spite of all those differences, stock returns have remained remarkably consistent. It's almost like there is a gravitational force that, regardless of any changes, always pulls stock returns back to their long-term average."

"So you're saying that, even though things could be different in the future, those differences won't matter?" interpreted one man. "How can you be certain?"

The instructor shook his head. "You can't be certain. Remember, we aren't seeking perfection, we are trying to maximize our odds of achieving our goals. History tells us that, for whatever reason, despite dramatic changes in the economy and financial markets, long-term equity returns have been remarkably consistent. While this could change, we have no good reason to think it will.

"Here is what this means for your personal financial management: if you can match the performance of the overall stock market, and the stock market returns its long-term average during the period you invest, you can expect to achieve about a 6.5% rate of return, in constant dollars, after paying fees and transaction costs."

Mark felt comfortable with stock investing, but not with that target. "That number seems pretty low. As I said, my goal for my stock investments is more like 15%. Even if you take inflation out, I'd still expect to earn more than 10% per year."

Mark was clearly not the only person with that viewpoint. Although everyone seemed aware of the risks of equity investing –

perhaps because they were so aware of those risks – people expected to earn very high returns from their equity investments.

Bruce spoke up next: "I tend to agree with Mark. I had thought the market average was higher than that, but even so, I try to beat the market when I invest. Even a small improvement over 6.5% would make a big difference over a long time."

"It sure would," agreed the instructor. "If you invested for 30 years, earning 8% per year instead of 6.5% per year would give you 50% more money at the end! It's pretty tempting. Your comment leads us to the second question I said we'd address: 'what equity securities to invest in.' Let's have a show of hands. How many of you currently own or have owned individual stocks?"

Most of the people in the class raised their hands. "I'm curious," said the instructor, "how do you decide which stock to purchase?"

One man answered quickly: "I hardly ever buy stocks. When I do, it's usually based on a tip from someone. You know, someone I trust might say that a certain stock is about to go up, and I should buy it. So I'll go out and buy a few shares."

Bruce followed a different approach. "I don't like relying on other people. I prefer to do my own research. In some ways it's a hobby, because I enjoy researching a stock, even reading the financial reports. I subscribe to a bunch of newsletters to get ideas, but I always do my own research before I buy anything."

One woman had a slightly different take: "I agree with Bruce about doing my own research, but I don't have the time to read financial reports. I work in the technology industry, so I encounter lots of small public companies in my work. I try to use that knowledge to my advantage. If I have positive first hand experience with a company, I'll buy its stock."

A number of stock-pickers still had their hands raised, ready to expound their strategy, but the instructor asked everyone to put their hands down. "We'll discuss the wisdom of these strategies in a moment. Before we do, let me ask if all of you are familiar with equity mutual funds?"

Again, most hands went up. "Good," said the instructor. "For those of you not familiar with equity mutual funds, they are similar the fixed income mutual funds we discussed earlier today, except that they invest in stocks. Equity mutual funds come in two basic varieties: actively managed funds, which try to exceed a stock market index, and index funds, which try to match a stock market index."

That description provoked a question from Jack: "Why would anyone want one of the index funds when they could choose a fund that beat the index?"

"That's an important question, and we'll spend considerable time answering it in a few minutes," responded the instructor. "I'll give you a shorthand answer now. An index fund can be a very useful tool because investing in one virtually guarantees that your equity investments will achieve the rate of return that the overall market achieves. Since we just explained that the overall market will most likely achieve a 6.5 – 7 percent rate of return over a long Time Horizon, you can be reasonably confident that investing in an equity index fund will give you about a 6.5% rate of return, after expenses."

"But if you are shooting for a higher return, an equity index fund would be a poor choice, right?" asked Jack.

"Right," agreed the instructor. "Mark and Bruce want to set their goal above the market average. They can't expect to achieve their goal with an index fund, so they would need to invest some other way."

"So if you are going to try to beat the market, you need to try to pick stocks that will earn more than 6.5% per year?" asked one man.

"Perhaps, but I want to question whether you should try to beat the market," said the instructor. "Your real objective is not to beat the market. Your real objective is to achieve your personal goals! The only reason to buy individual stocks would be to increase the likelihood that you could achieve your financial goals. Even if there were a high probability that you could earn more than 6.5% – and we will see soon that there isn't – the strong possibility of earning much less than 6.5% should scare you away from individual stocks."

Bruce was not in that camp yet. "Hang on a second. You agreed that even a small improvement in the rate of return makes a big difference in the long run. We clearly have a better chance of achieving our goals if our stocks earn 8% instead of 6.5%. If picking a few good stocks makes that possible, why shouldn't we do it?" he asked.

"He just told you why," piped in Andrea. "What if you're wrong about the stocks you pick? If you pick a few stocks and they go down instead of up, you could lose your college money."

"Can't you reduce that risk by diversification?" added Joe. "You need to own enough different stocks so that if one or two do poorly, they don't drag down your entire portfolio."

"That's true," agreed Mark. "You know I'm with Bruce in believing you can make money picking stocks, but I agree you need to be diversified, because you can't always guess right. Personally, I like to own between five and ten stocks at all times."

"Is that enough?" asked Andrea.

As usual, everyone turned to the instructor for technical questions. "Not really," he answered. "With five or ten stocks, you could have some pretty wild swings. You need to own twenty or thirty stocks for adequate diversification. Otherwise, you may earn your eight percent, but you could also endure very negative results."

"Well, if you need to own twenty stocks, that rules out most of the strategies people were talking about, doesn't it?" said Joe. "It's not like any of us have the time to research that many stocks and still keep our day job."

"That's certainly true," agreed the instructor. "That alone should kill the idea of investing in individual stocks. But, in case any of you are not convinced yet, and I suspect there are a few who are not, I'm going to twist the knife a little more. Do you know how many mutual funds and hedge funds there are investing in stocks right now?"

"There must be thousands," said Mitchell.

"Tens of thousands," corrected the instructor. "Each one employs squadrons of stock analysts. There are also thousands of analysts employed by brokerage firms. Add to that the managers of pension funds, foundations, and endowments. All these highly paid, intelligent professionals spend their entire days researching, evaluating, and selecting stocks. Do you really think that the information you see on CNBC, or read in a magazine or newspaper, or even a tip you hear from an employee of a company, is something that these professionals are not aware of?

"These professionals listen to all the company conference calls and read all the relevant financial information. They go to conferences where they meet personally with the management teams of the businesses they cover. Then they build very sophisticated financial models to analyze the impact of a wide variety of variables. As an individual, part-time investor, you have a huge information disadvantage."

The instructor's diatribe made an impact. While many of his earlier arguments appeared somewhat counterintuitive, this one looked obvious. Believing otherwise seemed like wishful thinking. Still, not everyone was ready to concede. Mark had at least one arrow left in his quiver. "I'm willing to admit what you say is true, but I still think I can do better than the market. Here's my advantage: most professional investors focus on short-term results. They must because their investors constantly measure their performance. I'm focused on the long-term. I can buy the out-of-favor stocks that the professionals have to avoid, and just wait until their true value becomes clear."

Mark's argument sounded surprisingly persuasive. Even with a short-term information disadvantage, could a investor with a long-term focus prosper? Mitchell didn't think so. "I don't accept that all professionals are short-term traders. Warren Buffet isn't a cult figure for nothing. I suspect there are truckloads of investors copying his strategy."

"But not with his success," said Jack. "I can speak from my own experience. I thought I was investing for the long term, but after my stocks were down for a couple years, and they had lost 90% of their value, I gave up and sold them."

"I agree," added another man thoughtfully. "I think of myself as a long term investor, but I can't stomach the losses. Maybe I'm not as long-term as I like to think."

"You aren't alone," said the instructor. "Amateur investors don't normally have the confidence to stick with their losers. And they shouldn't. There is a good chance their losers really are losers."

"I have to admit, you are starting to convince me," said Bruce. "The problem is, it just seems like figuring out which companies will be successful in the long run shouldn't be that hard. We all have a sense for what companies are good companies. We deal with them at work, we buy their products, we hear about them from our friends, and we read about them in the press. If we simply buy their stocks and hold onto them, shouldn't we make money? Why doesn't it work?"

"Good question," said the instructor. "Long term stock picking is harder than it seems. First, consider how far into the future you can reliably see? Can you guess which companies will be successful 30 years into the future?"

"Not a chance" answered Joe. "Lots of the best companies today didn't even exist 30 years ago."

"I agree," said Eric. "At best you can see a few years out. After that new technologies will change the world in totally unpredictable ways."

"Still," said Mark, "even if you only look out five years, you have a longer term focus than most everyone else."

"Doesn't matter," said the instructor. "Let's imagine you could accurately forecast the next five years. If your Time Horizon for your Retirement Fund is 30 years, you need to successfully pick a portfolio of stocks six different times! Every five years you need to successfully identify the top performing companies for the next five years. You are setting a very high bar for yourself."

"Sure, but if you can do it, you can do it," countered Mark.

"I don't think you, as an individual investor, can do it," said the instructor matter-of-factly. "Think about highly successful big companies like GE, IBM, ExxonMobil, Wal-Mart, or Pfizer, the ones who might seem most likely to retain their leadership five years from now. These conglomerates have multiple subsidiaries, often in very different industries. They operate globally, subject to a wide variety of competitive situations, some working in their favor, some against. Various government regulations and tax issues, all continually subject to change, materially impact them. I would suggest to you that even their top executives have little idea what their profits will be in five years. It is simply impossible for an individual investor to know enough about them to know how successful they'll be."

"Sure, that's true about the big companies," agreed Mark, "but I focus on smaller, more off-the-beaten-path businesses. They are much simpler to understand."

"True, but they have a variety of other risks. Small companies usually don't have the protected competitive positions that come with large scale. They often operate in newer industries that transform rapidly. Unfavorable transformations can have devastating impacts because small businesses don't have the protection of diversification among industries that larger businesses enjoy. Small companies also tend to be more dependent on one or a few key managers. For all these reasons and many others, while you may be more likely to be right about the future prospects of a small business, when you are wrong you could be very wrong."

The instructor could sense the impact of his argument. Still, he had one more key concept to impart: "Even if you reject everything I have said, even if you believe that you can accurately forecast a company's future profits, how would you recognize a bargain price to pay for that company's stock today?"

"I'm not sure what you mean," said Eric.

"Suppose that, in spite of all odds, you could consistently guess right about which companies will succeed in the future. You still might not make money investing in them. If other investors expect similar growth, today's stock price will incorporate those expectations."

"How do you know what growth other investors expect?" Eric asked.

"You don't. You can try to compute the market's growth expectations for a stock using the price per share, the current earnings per share, and the discount rate, which is the rate of return investors would expect on that particular stock. You can look up the price per share and earnings per share, but you must estimate the discount rate."

"How do you do that?"

"It's not easy. If you are good at math and have read some finance textbooks, you can arrive at a reasonable range. Be aware that a small underestimate of the discount rate can lead to a large underestimate of the assumed growth rate, and vice versa."

"I just don't get it – this is way too complicated!" Eric gave up, throwing up his hands.

"Yes, and I am simplifying endlessly. I am ignoring dividends, I am ignoring the pattern the growth rate will take, I am ignoring the question of what the price earnings ratio will be in five years when you want to sell the stock. The point of this discussion is to make you believe, deep in your bones, that you, as an individual investor, cannot reasonably expect to exceed the performance of professionals in picking long-term stock winners, and that it would be foolish for you to try."

At this point, as he surveyed the room, the instructor realized with satisfaction that no one continued to argue for owning individual stocks. Still, he had one more topic to cover. After a pause, he began again: "Persuading you not to buy individual stocks is half my battle. For equities, you must use mutual funds. Remember the two types, index funds and actively managed funds? Earlier, Jack asked why we would choose an index fund instead of an actively managed fund whose sole purpose is earning more than the index. It does seem paradoxical to choose an index fund instead of a fund specifically intended to earn more than that index. But let me tip my hand – that is exactly what I recommend. "

"Why?" asked Bruce. "Didn't you just show all the advantages professional investors have over individuals? Can't we benefit from those advantages by investing in funds managed by those professionals?

"I don't think so," responded Joe. "I know I've read that most funds fail to beat the S&P500 index."

"I've heard that, too," said Andrea, "but it doesn't make sense to me. The sole purpose of a mutual fund is to beat the index. I just can't believe that most of them fail."

"I can," said Mitchell. "Professional fund managers have all the same challenges individuals have. I doubt they can foresee the future better than we can."

"Even if they could," added the instructor, "it would be mathematically impossible for most of them to beat the market index. The market index measures the results of all the stocks in the market. Professional investors own the vast majority of those stocks. The average result of all the professional investors has to equal the result of the market index."

The participants thought about that for a minute. Bruce said: "Equal isn't the same as worse. If the average fund's results are equal to the market index, why is it better to choose an index fund?"

"The results are equal before subtracting the fees," answered the instructor. "Actively managed funds normally have higher fees, often 1.5% per year higher. Those fees will reduce your rate of return to around 5% per year instead of 6.5%."

"Even if most funds do worse than the index," countered Bruce, "some certainly beat it. You always find stories in the financial press about managers who have beaten the market by whopping amounts. Why not invest in those funds?"

"I agree with Bruce," said James. "The fact that most funds don't beat the index doesn't matter if your fund does beat it. Unless you believe that successful funds are just lucky, choosing a very good fund and sticking with it seems like a good strategy."

"James is right," added Mark. "Some people are simply smarter and more hardworking than others. Those are the people whose funds will succeed, and they are the ones whose funds we should buy."

"But how do you know how smart or hardworking your fund managers are?" countered Mitchell. "You never meet them. You don't know why they pick their stocks. You don't see their work habits. You don't know anything about them except their track record."

"Well, if you accept that the smarter and more hard working managers will do best, than seeing their track record ought to be sufficient," answered Mark, a bit defiantly.

"Unfortunately, it isn't," interjected the instructor. "In fact, choosing the funds with the best track record over the last few years is close to the worst possible investment strategy you can follow. Stock sectors move in and out of favor somewhat cyclically. If growth stocks have done well for a few years, funds that emphasize growth stocks will have a strong track record during that period. If you invest in those funds based upon that track record, you will likely suffer below average returns over the next few years, as growth stocks fall out of favor."

"That sounds like my experience with technology stocks," commented Jack. "I bought them after they had been going through the roof for a few years, and it didn't take long before they were in a free fall. The mutual funds buying those stocks didn't do any better than I did."

"I understand what you are all saying, but I'm not ready to concede on this yet," said Mark. "Maybe you can't look at a fund's track record for the last few years and be sure its success means it has a great manager. But surely over ten years, if a fund has been consistently outstanding, you would have sufficient evidence of exceptional management."

"I could concede that and it still wouldn't help you buy actively managed funds," said the instructor. "Very few funds have a ten-year track record of consistent success. Most of those that do will be totally closed to new investors or have a minimum investment too high for all but the wealthiest individuals. You probably won't find any you can buy.

"Even if you can find one, you shouldn't invest in it. A fund with a great ten-year track record that remains open for your investment will have trouble duplicating its prior performance. Its assets will have grown astronomically, making it unable to use many of the strategies that made it successful when it was smaller. Plus, the fund's manager will by now be very wealthy. He or she may burn out and coast or even retire. Before you realize that the fund will never again duplicate its prior success, you could lose a lot of money."

By this point, the resistance had mostly evaporated. Many of the participants had begun the day psychologically invested in their various strategies for beating the market. They didn't give up those strategies easily. In the end, however, they could not ignore the persuasiveness of the instructor's logic. The instructor turned to the flip chart and wrote:

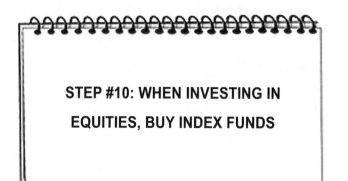

STEP #10: WHEN INVESTING IN

EQUITIES, BUY INDEX FUNDS

"I have to say," said Eric, "that what you are telling us is comforting. There's much less stress in putting our money in an index fund than picking stocks or mutual funds. I prefer not having to research funds. Especially in my 401k, where my choices are limited, I never felt comfortable with the funds I've selected, so I probably changed them far too often."

"You touched another important point, Eric," said the instructor. "I've been demonstrating that the Investment Risk in choosing stocks and actively managed equity mutual funds is unacceptably high. An equal benefit from avoiding them is eliminating Behavioral Risk. Buying and holding index funds takes Behavioral Risk out of the picture. People tend to do grave damage to themselves when they get overly involved investing their equities. Frequently buying and selling individual stocks compounds the problems involved in selecting them. Switching between mutual funds has the same disastrous effects. When investing in equities, simply determine how much money you have to invest, put all of that money into an index fund, and leave it there until it is time to switch it out of equities and into a fixed income investment."

"That sounds simple, but we still need to know how much to invest in equities and when to switch it. We haven't learned that yet, have we?" asked Andrea.

"No, but we will over the next two weeks. We are now ready to discuss saving for college and saving for retirement, the two main long term objectives. We will start on saving for college when you return next week."

BIG STEP FOUR

Save for College

CHAPTER ELEVEN

Understanding College Financial Aid

On his ride to the seminar for the fourth session, Joe wondered if he would find much worthwhile this day. The first three sessions had exceeded his hopes. He possessed renewed confidence in his financial future. He had begun to save money, making his first month's payments on his debt reduction plan. He foresaw creating an Auto Fund in two years and a Home Fund two years after that. He knew exactly how he would invest the money in his funds. When he thought of the long-term, he thought mainly of his retirement account. Today' session, geared as it would be toward saving for college, held little interest for him at this stage in his life.

The sound of laughter greeted Joe as he entered the classroom before the session began. A crowd had gathered around Mitchell as he told the story of the 'college tour' he had recently taken with his oldest son: "We drove everywhere. I honestly think that boy has no idea what kind of school he wants to attend. We went to state schools with 50,000 students and private schools with 2,000. We must have gone to twelve colleges in a week. One of them he added to our itinerary because he saw a billboard for it on the interstate."

"I think you're lucky," Bruce commented when Mitchell had finished his story. "He'll probably be happy wherever he goes. My daughters are only fourteen and they have already made up their minds about what college they're going to. If they don't get in, they'll be devastated. And if they do get in, that could be even worse, because I don't know if we could afford it."

"I can see how that would be stressful," Mitchell sympathized. I don't know what's worse. We're less than a year from the start of school, and I have no idea whether I have enough money saved. His younger brother is only a year behind him, too. If they go to state schools, I think I'm fine, but if they go to private schools, it could be a real stretch."

"Have you thought of telling them they have to go to state schools?" asked one of the older members of the class. "That's what I did with my kids. I told them there was no way we could afford to send them to a private school. I wanted to keep them close to home, anyway."

"I've thought about it," Mitchell said, shaking his head, "but I don't want to do it. I loved college. I want them to go somewhere they'll love. I feel like it's my responsibility to give them that opportunity."

The instructor came into the room and asked everyone to take their seats. He wore a large smile, as he enjoyed this particular class and had looked forward to it since the first day of the seminar.

"At the risk of setting expectations too high," began the instructor, "I suspect many of you, especially those who have young children or do not even have children yet, will look back on today's session as the most valuable. For many parents, the uncertainty inherent in saving for their children's education causes substantial stress. I suspect many of you feel that stress. Let's begin by hearing from some of you about how you approach saving for college."

Andrea spoke first. "All along, I've been most excited about this session. Saving for college always worries me. My daughter is ten, so she has eight more years before she starts college. I've been saving as much as I can, but I don't know if it will be enough. Not knowing is the worst part."

"I agree that not knowing is the worst," added Mitchell. "If you knew how much money you needed, college would cause much less stress. My oldest applied to seven different schools. The most expensive cost almost $40,000 per year. The least expensive cost only $14,000 per year. How much do I need to have saved?"

Mark was nodding sympathetically. "I'm going to be in the same boat when my kids are ready for college, too. I've got six kids to send through college. Can I afford private school for all of them? I don't know. Like Andrea said, I've been saving as much as I can, but I don't know if I'll have enough. I guess it will come down to how much financial aid I can get, and who knows what that will be? It's enough to drive you crazy."

Eric had a different concern. "Listening to everyone just makes me more scared. I'm already worried, because I keep reading that college costs are rising so rapidly. With our young kids, it will be fourteen or more years before we start paying for college. What will it cost then? Can college tuition keep increasing forever?"

Sally added to his thought: "We've been trying to save for college, but its hard. We're both early in our careers, so we hope to earn more in the future. Hopefully we'll have more money to save for college then, because right now we don't have much. If our income doesn't grow as we expect, what then? Do our kids not go to college?"

Everyone looked gloomy. Despite the instructor's promise that this class would energize everyone, it had begun on a sour note. The instructor sought to lighten their moods: "Is anyone surprised by this conversation?"

No one seemed to be.

"Of course not. I promise you that by the end of today you will feel entirely different about the prospect of saving for college. We will handle the uncertainty by providing you enough information that you can feel confident that your college savings program will succeed. Before you leave this session, you will have learned how to determine how much money you must save each month to ensure that you will have enough in your College Fund to pay for college."

He stood up and walked to the flip chart. "I'm going to list the four main questions which cause uncertainty about saving for college. Then, one by one, we will address each of them, and you will learn how to answer them for your own unique circumstances. You will then be able to calculate a goal for your College Fund, which we'll refer to as your College Fund Target, in much the same way you did for your Auto Fund and your Home Fund."

QUESTIONS IMPACTING SAVING FOR COLLEGE

- How much financial aid will you receive?
- What college will your child attend?
- What will you be earning when your child matriculates?
- How much will college costs rise before your child matriculates?

"Let's begin with the first question: how much financial aid will you receive? For most of you, this question is the starting point for calculating your College Fund Target. You need to understand how college financial aid works before you consider your savings requirements. Are any of you familiar with how college financial aid works?"

"Sure," answered one man, "my three kids are out of college by now, so I guess I'm something of an expert. You fill out some very detailed forms listing your income and your assets, and the college tells you how much you have to pay. They also tell you how much of your aid will be grants, which are never repaid, and how much will be loans, which your child will have to pay back."

"Are the forms the same for all schools?" asked one woman.

"There are two basic sets of forms," answered the instructor. The primary one is created by the U.S. Government. Many schools, especially the more expensive ones, also require that you fill out a different set created by the College Board – the organization that administers the SAT. A few schools also have supplemental financial aid forms unique to their school, but most don't. All the forms require you to provide specific information that is plugged into a formula.

"Now, pay attention. It's very important that you understand that the formula calculates a single number: your Expected Family Contribution. We'll call it the EFC. The EFC is, approximately, the amount you will pay for college each year."

"Do both sets of forms work the same way?" asked the woman.

"They do. They request very similar information, and each will calculate an EFC. With few exceptions, the EFC calculated by each method will be very close. Our examples will use the government methodology because most colleges use it."

"Even if the schools use the same forms, don't the schools have some discretion in deciding how much financial aid to give you?" asked Mitchell.

"They do, but most schools' financial aid packages won't deviate too far from the calculated EFC, unless the school is having serious financial problems."

"I'm not sure how this works," said Andrea. "You fill out these forms, which determine your EFC. That's how much you pay? What about the cost of the school? Where does that come in?"

"That is the beauty of college financial aid," answered the instructor. "For most people, the cost of college does not affect how much you pay!" He pointed to Question #2 on the flip chart: 'What College Will Your Child Attend?' Your EFC determines how much you pay. Financial aid makes up the difference between your EFC and your college's costs. Since financial aid covers any costs over the EFC, it often doesn't matter what school your child attends."

"Are you saying it costs the same amount regardless of where your child goes to school?" asked Andrea, surprised.

"Believe it or not, that is often the case, especially for people with lower EFCs. For example, for a family with an EFC of $8,000, they will pay approximately $8,000 whether their child attends an in-state public school or an expensive private school, as both schools would cost more than their EFC."

"That wasn't the case for me, though," said one woman. Our EFC was about $25,000, which is higher than in-state tuition. So, while we didn't get any financial aid for our son, who went to the state school, we still spent less paying for his college than we did for our daughter, who went to an Ivy League school."

"That highlights an important point," said the instructor. "The EFC represents, approximately, the maximum you will have to pay for college. People with high EFCs can spend less than that amount if their children choose less expensive schools.

"Let's do some math and this will become clear. I will take you through some examples so that you can see how to estimate your EFC. He went to the flip chart and flipped over the page with the four questions on it. On the next page he wrote:

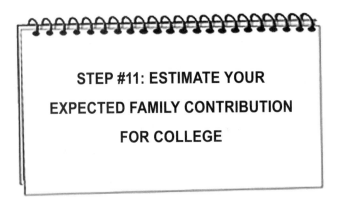

STEP #11: ESTIMATE YOUR

EXPECTED FAMILY CONTRIBUTION

FOR COLLEGE

"Mitchell," he said, "if you don't mind, we'll use you as our example."

"Sure," said Mitchell happily, "I could use the help."

"Great. The EFC calculation utilizes four items: parents' income, parents' assets, students' income, and students' assets. We will ignore the student portion. If your children have income or assets, the formula expects them to contribute the majority of their money to pay for college. Student income and assets will raise your EFC and correspondingly reduce the amount of financial aid you will receive."

"Does that mean we shouldn't encourage our children to work and save for college?" asked Bruce. "I've been telling my kids for years that they need to save their money if they want to go to college."

"It depends whether you will be eligible for financial aid. If your income and assets are too large for you to receive financial aid, your children's contributions to paying for their education will reduce the burden on you. But if you are eligible for aid, your children's contributions will reduce the amount of aid you receive. The amount you need to have in your College Fund will not be significantly less than if your children contributed nothing.

"Even so," countered Bruce, "reducing the amount of aid could reduce the amount of debt my kids will have when they finish college. I also think teaching kids to save money for college is an important message."

The instructor held up his hands defensively. "I am certainly not telling you that having your children save money for college is unnecessary or unwise. I'm only making the point that having your children save will not reduce the amount that *you* need to save. To estimate your EFC, therefore, you can assume your children will have zero income and assets. Understand?"

There were no more comments, so he continued: "Your income plays the major role in determining your EFC. Mitchell, what is your gross income? By the way, gross income means your total income before taxes. We've mostly used net income in this class, but for calculating your EFC, we need your gross income."

"Does investment income count?" asked Mitchell.

"Yes, all income counts. Salary, wages, bonuses, investment income, everything."

"This year it is roughly $120,000," Mitchell replied. "Do the formulas use an average of your income over a period of years?"

"No, they use a single year."

The instructor passed out a worksheet showing, in detail, how to estimate your EFC.[5]

He continued speaking as he passed it out: "For each school year, the EFC calculation uses your income earned in the most recently ended calendar year. The EFC calculation estimates your after tax income for that year and takes a few deductions based on how many parents work, how many children are in the family, and how many children are in college. The resulting amount is called Available Income. This amount is deemed available to be spent on college bills. For you, with $120,000 gross income, I estimate your Available Income at $56,000.

"Next, the calculation increases Available Income by 12% of the parents' assets."

"Are all assets included in that calculation?" Mitchell asked.

"No, many assets don't count. Assets held in a 401k, IRA, or other retirement account don't count, nor does the value of your home. For most of you, assets will have little impact. In fact, the assets that will matter most tend to be the very savings in the College Fund which has been dedicated for this purpose. Mitchell, can you give me a rough estimate of your assets? A ballpark guess is fine."

"I'd guess $100,000," said Mitchell.

---

[5] The worksheet to estimate your EFC is included in Appendix 1. For a more detailed spreadsheet, see www.dougwarshauer.com.

"Okay.   The formula will deduct an amount, in your case $55,500, from that number, multiply the remainder by 12%, and add the total to your Available Income. After that calculation, your Available Income is now $61,000.

"The final step in the calculation is translating your Available Income to your EFC. The formula works like graduated income tax: you are "taxed" at a rate of 22% of the first $14,500 of Available Income. The rate quickly climbs and caps out at 47% of all Available Income over $29,300. Applying that formula for Mitchell, I calculate an EFC of about $23,000.

LET'S DO THE MATH

Gross Salary	$120,000
Available Income[6]	$56,000
Assessable Assets	$100,000
Asset Allowance[7]	$55,500
Net Assessable Assets	$44,500
Assessment Rate	12%
Contribution from Assets	$5,340
Adjusted Available Income	$61,290
(Available Income plus Contribution from Assets)	
Expected Contribution	**$23,000**

The class looked at the calculations. Although they could follow the process, the calculations remained obscure.

"I see what you're doing," said Bruce, "but how do we do it for ourselves?"

---

[6] Gross income is reduced by federal income taxes, social security taxes, an allowance for state taxes, and a couple other allowances based on the number of parents working, the number of family members, and the number of family members in college.
[7] Asset allowance based on the age of the oldest parent and whether the family is a one-parent or two-parent family

"Use the worksheet I passed out," answered the instructor, "It's not very difficult. But don't worry about doing your own calculations yet. Right now I just want you to understand the process.

"So you get a better feel for how this formula works, let's pretend Mitchell's numbers were a little different. If his income were ten thousand higher, and his assets were the same, his EFC would be $26,000 instead of $23,000. Of that extra $10,000 in income, about $3,000 goes to pay for college. If his income were $170,000 instead of $120,000, he would have an EFC of $39,000."

"Isn't that getting to the point where you won't get any financial aid? How many colleges cost more than $39,000?" asked Mark.

"I know some do," answered one man. "I paid over $40,000 last year."

"$38,000 is close to the average for a private college right now," said the instructor. "Naturally, some cost more than average. I think the point is well taken, though, that if you have a gross income of $160,000 or more, and you have only one child in college, you will get little if any financial aid. But if you have two children in college, you could get aid. Mark, you said you have six children, right?"

"That's right."

"So you may be eligible for aid, even though you have a pretty high income."

"I hope so," said Mark, "I'm going to need it."

"Let's look at one more example. Andrea, you said you were very concerned about paying for college. Do you mind if we use you?"

"Not at all," she replied.

"Good. I need to know your gross income and your assets."

Andrea was ready with her numbers. "My gross income is $60,000, and my assets are $20,000."

"Just to remind me, you are single, with one child, right?"

"Right," said Andrea.

"That has a small impact on the calculation, as it affects a couple of deductions to your income and assets." He made a few calculations, then looked up. "Your EFC is $7,000." He wrote the number on the flip chart.

"Andrea's EFC is well below the average cost of an in-state public school. For her, a private school will not cost more than a public school. Regardless of where her daughter goes to school, Andrea will pay, approximately, her EFC.

"Let's make a couple of modifications again. Suppose here income were only $50,000. Her EFC falls to $5,000. Drop her income to $30,000 and the EFC falls all the way to $1,000. This is the level below which families have to pay very little for college."

LET'S DO THE MATH

Gross Salary	$60,000
Available Income[8]	$26,000
Assessable Assets	$20,000
Asset Allowance[9]	$21,500
Net Assessable Assets	$0
Assessment Rate	12%
Contribution from Assets	$0
Adjusted Available Income	$26,000
(Available Income plus Contribution from Assets)	
Expected Contribution	$7,000

"So if you earn less than $30,000, college is almost free?" asked one man.

---

[8] Gross income is reduced by federal income taxes, social security taxes, an allowance for state taxes, and a couple other allowances based on the number of parents working, the number of family members, and the number of family members in college.

[9] Asset allowance based on the age of the oldest parent and whether the family is a one-parent or two-parent family

"Well, it is not free because the student will end up with substantial loans, and will probably need to participate in work-study programs. But the parents will not be expected to contribute much. Most people with incomes below $30,000 do not need to save for college for their children. Thirty thousand dollars doesn't go far in the U.S. today. People who earn $30,000 or less will have a very hard time saving any of their net income. Staying out of debt is a reasonable goal for people at that income level."

"I understand your calculations," said Joe, "but all this depends on financial aid programs remaining the same indefinitely. What if the formulas or even the programs change in the future?"

"Many things could change," agreed the instructor. "The grants and loans and work-study programs in existence today could change, leaving your children with more or less debt after college. Also, the EFC formula which I have shown you could change. It could be dropped entirely, though that seems doubtful. Does anyone here expect financial aid for college to disappear entirely?"

No one seemed to think that was too likely.

"These financial aid formulas have been around for a while. Colleges and the government may tweak them, but the basic principal of linking an expected family contribution to income and assets seems highly likely to remain in place. You can have confidence that a savings plan based upon today's rules will serve you well, especially if you modify your plan if and when any significant changes are made to financial aid formulas in the future.

"It's a good time for a break. We discussed the first two questions: how financial aid works and what college your child will attend. After the break, we'll discuss how to look into the future to handle potential changes in your earnings and in college costs before your child reaches college age. Then you'll be ready to determine your College Fund Target."

CHAPTER TWELVE

Setting a College Fund Target

A s everyone returned from the break, the instructor immediately began the discussion. "Let's review what we've covered so far today. We started by listing four questions. The difficulty of answering those questions makes saving for college hazardous. We thoroughly addressed the most important question – how financial aid formulas determine the Expected Family Contribution. In the process, we also addressed the second question – the impact of college selection – which turns out not to matter much for people with low Expected Family Contributions.

"If your child is college age now, you have all the information you need. The two remaining questions reflect the impact of changes between the present and the time your child reaches college age. The third question applies to changes in your income, which will affect your eligibility for financial aid as well as your ability to contribute to your college fund, and the fourth question applies to changes in the cost of college. Let's begin by discussing the third question, the question of what your earnings will be when your children are in college."

"That's one I think I can predict. Unless my boss is planning to surprise me with a big raise, my income next year will be about what it is now," said Mitchell, a bit hopelessly. "I bet changing incomes have a bigger impact on the young folks in the group like Eric and Sally or Jack and Isabel."

"You're right," agreed the instructor, "they do."

"I was wondering about this issue as you presented Andrea's example," said Eric. "She has eight years before her child goes to college. Sally and I have even longer. How can we know how much we will be earning then? If the financial aid formula utilizes your net income from the year before your child starts college, how can we estimate our EFC? If our earnings increase, using our current income will make us overestimate the amount of aid we'll receive. That could mislead us into saving too little."

Eric voiced a question that had occurred to many people when the instructor had first explained the financial aid calculation. They looked to him for a response.

"Eric is right," said the instructor. Most of you, especially those with young children, hope and expect to earn more when your children reach college age than you earn today. Your financial aid level will depend upon your future income, not your current income. Obviously, you need to predict your future income."

"You'd need to be a fortune teller to do that," said Bruce skeptically. "I wish I knew what I would make in the future. It depends on so many things: my performance reviews, whether I get promoted, how my company does. I've only got four years before my kids start college, and I have no idea what I'll earn then. How could someone as young as Eric know?"

Bruce's comment, like Eric's, made sense. The group felt in their bones that saving for college was a crapshoot. As the members of the group voiced explanations for its impossibility, they felt themselves physically in agreement. Although the explanation of the financial aid process had made some progress in building their confidence, the instructor knew he had a long way to go.

"I can see by your body language that Bruce is not the only one who feels that way," he told them. "Fortunately, you don't need to be a very accurate fortune teller. First, let me show you how to predict your income in the future, then I'll explain why it doesn't matter much whether your prediction is accurate or not."

He could tell that, in at least recognizing their concern, he'd calmed them for the moment, so he continued, "Most people earn more money as their career progresses, especially as their children approach college age. Their increased income results from two factors, inflationary increases and merit increases. We can separate a person's raise into those two components. If inflation is 2%, and you receive a 3% raise that year, we would say that you received an inflationary increase of 2% and a merit increase of 1%.

"Because of inflation, almost every job pays more today than the same job did twenty years ago. The salary, for example, of a first-year lawyer is far higher today than it was twenty years ago, even though a first-year lawyer today has no more experience than a first-year lawyer had twenty years ago. Inflation has caused first-year lawyer salaries to rise. Of course it's impossible, but if someone had been a first-year lawyer twenty years ago and remained a first-year lawyer today, he would perceive that he'd earned raises consistently over the intervening years.

"In reality, the first-year lawyer of twenty years ago is no longer a first-year lawyer. He has twenty years of experience and has likely progressed to the senior levels of the firm. He now earns far more than the current first-year lawyers. The difference between his earnings and the earnings of the current first-year lawyers represent the merit increases he has earned during his career. On average, most people earn a merit increase of 2-3% per year, in addition to their inflationary increase.

"Let's do some math to see how this impacts income over time. Andrea, let's update our projection of your EFC by estimating your earnings when your daughter begins college. You have a ten year old daughter, right, so you have eight years before college for her?"

"Yes, that's right, she's in fourth grade now."

"Good. The first thing you need to do, before doing the EFC calculation we discussed earlier, is estimate your merit increases over the next eight years. This will tell you your income, in today's dollars, when your daughter reaches college age."

Jack's hand went up. "Why do we estimate her income in today's dollars? Isn't inflation important?"

"Ignoring inflation makes everything simpler. By ignoring inflation, we can use today's college costs and today's financial aid formulas. We can also use the after-inflation investment return expectations that we discussed last week. We'll consider inflation separately in a few minutes, when we get to Question #4. Everyone with me?"

They seemed to be. Despite the complexity of the subject, the interest level kept people intently focused on the discussion.

"Andrea, let's assume you have an average merit salary increase of 3% per year for the next eight years. That's a bit above average, but, for estimating your EFC, it's better to err on the high side."

He stood up and went to the flip chart. "Here is a formula for calculating your earnings when your child reaches college age. It is a simple formula, but it requires the use of an exponent." He wrote the formula:

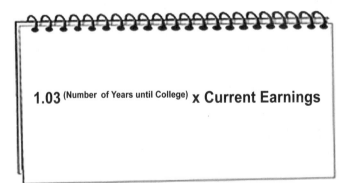

$$1.03^{\text{(Number of Years until College)}} \times \textbf{Current Earnings}$$

"Since Andrea's daughter has eight years until college, the 'Number of Years until College' is eight. 1.03^8 means multiplying

1.03 x 1.03 x 1.03 x 1.03 x 1.03 x 1.03 x 1.03 x 1.03. 1.03^8 equals 1.27. That means that eight years from now, Andrea will earn 1.27 times her current earnings. Her current earnings are $60,000, so in eight years she can expect to earn about $76,000. Do you all follow this? You can do this calculation on any pocket calculator or computer."

"I see you multiplied 1.03 by itself eight times. Why eight times?" asked one man.

"Because Andrea's daughter has eight years before college. Andrea has eight years to earn merit pay increases, and each year's merit increase will compound the impact of the previous years' pay increases."

"Can you explain why you used 1.03? I'm not sure I understood that part," asked another man.

"Yes," said the instructor. "The number 1.03 represents the 3% merit raises that Andrea expects to receive for the next eight years. If Andrea expected only 2% raises, than we would use 1.02 instead of 1.03."

"Does it really matter whether you use 1.02 or 1.03? Can 1% make a difference?"

"It matters for people with younger children. For Mitchell, the difference between a 2% or 3% raise in the next year means little. But for Andrea, it matters somewhat, and for someone who begins saving when their child is born, it matters greatly. Had Andrea expected a 2% raise, her income in eight years would be only about $70,000. To show you the difference, I will calculate her EFC in eight years assuming 3% raises, and again assuming 2% raises. Based on an income of $76,000, Andrea's EFC will be approximately $13,000. Had she only received 2% raises, her income in eight years would only be $70,000 and her EFC would be approximately $11,000.

LET'S DO THE MATH

Andrea with 3% merit pay increases

Gross Salary	today $60,000
Number of Years until College	8
Annual merit increases	3%
Salary multiplier (1.03^8)	1.27
Gross Salary in 8 Years	$76,000
Available Income	$37,000
Assessable Assets[10]	$50,000
Asset Allowance	$21,500
Net Assessable Assets	$28,500
Assessment Rate	12%
Contribution from Assets	$3,420
Adjusted Available Income	$40,420
(Available Income plus Contribution from Assets)	
Expected Contribution	$13,000

Andrea with 2% merit pay increases

Gross Salary	today $60,000
Number of Years until College	8
Annual merit increases	2%
Salary multiplier (1.02^8)	1.17
Gross Salary in 8 Years	$70,000
Available Income	$32,000
Assessable Assets	$50,000
Asset Allowance	$21,500
Net Assessable Assets	$28,500
Assessment Rate	12%
Contribution from Assets	$3,420
Adjusted Available Income	$35,420
(Available Income plus Contribution from Assets)	
Expected Contribution	$11,000

---

[10] Assumes she accumulates $50,000 in assets by the time her daughter is college age, compared to the $20,000 she has today.

"Doesn't that make the whole exercise questionable," asked Bruce. "You said before that you don't need to be a good fortune teller, but Andrea's calculations prove that small changes in the amount her earnings grow have a big impact on how much financial aid she'll get. It seems you need to be an extremely good fortune teller."

"It does seem that way, doesn't it?" said the instructor. "If Andrea estimates that her earnings will grow at 3%, and they grow either faster or slower, she will need either more or less money saved for college than she initially thought she would. But this isn't a big problem. Does anyone see why?"

Silence. People studied what he'd put on the board. Andrea suggested tentatively, "I think I see that it's not a problem, because if I earn less than the 3% raises I predicted, I will receive more financial aid than I expected. I'll have more money in my College Fund than I ultimately need."

"Good," said the instructor. "That's the easy part. The harder part is the case where your earnings grow *faster* than you predicted."

"Why is that harder?" asked Andrea.

"Because the increase in your income will reduce the amount of aid you receive. You must modify your College Fund Target whenever you get an unexpectedly large raise. You may need to devote a substantial chunk of your increased earnings to your College Fund. That is why I recommend using 3%, which is a little above average, as your expected merit increase."

"Are you saying that it doesn't matter if your predications are wrong, because your savings plan self-corrects?" said one woman.

"It doesn't self-correct, you have to adjust your savings yourself," corrected the instructor. "But it's not difficult to do if you stay on top of it, and you will have the financial resources to do it."

He turned to the flip chart and wrote:

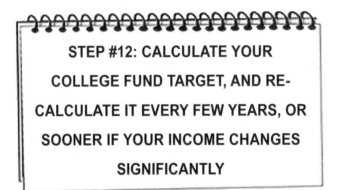

STEP #12: CALCULATE YOUR COLLEGE FUND TARGET, AND RE-CALCULATE IT EVERY FEW YEARS, OR SOONER IF YOUR INCOME CHANGES SIGNIFICANTLY

He paused for a moment. "We are now on the threshold of determining your College Fund Target. All you need to do is multiply your EFC by the *number of years you will have children in college*."

He paused again. "Listen carefully to what I said. Multiply your EFC by the number of years you will have children in college. If you have one child, multiply your EFC by four. If you have two children who will not overlap in college, you will have children in college eight different years. Multiply your EFC by eight. If you have children who are two school years apart, they will overlap two years, so you will only have children in college six different years. Multiply your EFC by six.

"Bruce, with your twins you are in luck: you will pay little if any more for two children than you would for one. Twins are the great bargain of the college financial aid system."

Bruce, who was not aware of that fact, looked stunned. And happy. "Are you certain?" he asked.

"I am. If your children attend private schools that use the College Board method, you will pay slightly more than you would if you had only one child. For schools that use the government method, you'll pay almost exactly the same for two children as you would for one. Let's take a quick look back at Andrea's and Mitchell's numbers so you can see this in action. Andrea's EFC is expected to be $13,000.

She has one child, so she needs to multiply $13,000 by four. Her College Fund Target is $52,000.

"Mitchell has two children only one school year apart, so he has three overlapping years. He will have five years with children in college. His EFC is about $23,000. Multiply that by five, and he needs a College Fund Target of $115,000."

LET'S DO THE MATH

Mitchell's College Fund Calculation

EFC	$23,000
Number of Children	2
Years of College Per Child	x4
Total College Years	8
Overlapping Years	-3
Total Unique Years with Children in College	5
College Fund Target	**$115,000**
(5 x $23,000)	

"Isn't it possible Mitchell will need less than that, if one or both of his boys go to an in-state public school?" asked Joe.

"That's exactly right. During the years they overlap, he will almost certainly pay his EFC, as $23,000 will be less than the sum of the two colleges' costs. But in the other two years, when only one child is in college, he could pay less than his EFC. In-state public schools costs currently average about $16,000. He'll save about $7,000 if one child chooses a state school, and $14,000 if they both do."

"So if I were to limit them to choosing a state school, I could reduce my College Fund Target from $115,000 to $101,000," proposed Mitchell.

"That's right," replied the instructor. "We have one major topic left. We need to discuss how people who don't expect to receive financial aid should calculate their College Fund Target."

"Isn't that easier?" asked Jack. Can't they just multiply the average cost of college by the number of years they'll have children in college?"

"You're missing one step," the instructor answered. "You need to address college price inflation. Remember, everyone, this was our fourth question. It is only relevant for people who don't expect financial aid. For everyone else, changes in the price of colleges won't affect how much you must pay, they'll affect how much aid you receive. For people who will pay for college on their own, here is how to take college inflation into account."

He returned to the flip chart. "This is a formula that should look familiar, as it is similar to the formula for predicting your income when your child reaches college age." He wrote:

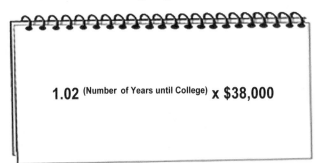

$$1.02^{\text{(Number of Years until College)}} \times \$38,000$$

"Let's pretend Andrea earned so much money she had no chance of receiving financial aid."

"I like this game!" Andrea said enthusiastically.

"She still has eight years before her daughter goes to college," continued the instructor, "so the Number of years until College is eight. 1.02 represents the amount that college costs will probably rise in excess of inflation. It is akin to her merit pay increase, which is the amount by which her income will rise in excess of inflation.

"1.02^8 equals 1.02 x 1.02 x 1.02 x 1.02 x 1.02 x 1.02 x 1.02 x 1.02, which equals 1.17. In eight years, we expect colleges will cost 1.17 times more than they do today. Now, assume Andrea's daughter will attend a private school –"

"We're not pretending anymore," interjected Andrea sarcastically.

"Maybe not, but remember, Real Andrea is protected by financial aid, Rich Andrea is not," reminded the instructor. "The average private school today costs $38,000. Multiply that by 1.17. In eight years, in today's dollars, the average private school will cost approximately $45,000. Without financial aid, Rich Andrea will need her College Fund to cover that entire price tag. Multiplying $45,000 by four equals $180,000, which would be the College Fund Target for Rich Andrea.

"Finally, let's imagine Rich Andrea had a second child, two years younger than the first. The second child won't be college age for ten years, so the formula: $1.02^{10} \times 38,000$ produces an annual cost of approximately 46,000. If Rich Andrea's EFC were $50,000, she actually would receive financial aid for the two years the children were both in school. Therefore, her College Fund Target would be the sum of $45,000 x 2 (older child in school alone), $50,000 x 2 (overlapping years), and $46,000 x 2 (younger child in school alone), for a total of $282,000.

LET'S DO THE MATH

One Child

Current Average Private College Cost	$38,000
Expected Annual Increase	1.02
Years Until College	8
Expected Cost of College	$44,523
(1.02^8 x $36,000$)	
Years of College	x 4
College Fund Target	**$178,092**

Two Children

Cost with older child alone	$44,523
Number of Years	x 2
Required Fund for first 2 years	**$89,046**
Cost with two children together (EFC)	$50,000
Overlapping Years	x 2
Required Fund for middle 2 years	**$100,000**
Current Annual Private College Cost	$38,000
Expected Annual Increase	1.02
Years Until College	10
Expected Cost of College	$46,322
$(1.02^{10}$ x $36,000)$	
Cost with younger child alone	$46,322
Number of Years	x 2
Required Fund for final 2 years	**$92,644**
College Fund Target	**$281,690**

"Although this may seem complicated, it's not. You are simply estimating your cost for each year you will have a child in college. For each individual year, you need to determine whether you will receive financial aid. If you will, use your EFC. If you will not, use the expected future cost of college. Then total up the years to calculate your College Fund Target.

"Let's break now. When we return, we'll discuss how to invest your College Fund so that you maximize your chances of achieving your target amount when your children reach college age."

CHAPTER THIRTEEN

Investing Your College Fund

After the break, the instructor held up his hand patiently waiting for their attention. At last, he spoke: "We covered a lot of material already today. I suspect it hasn't all sunk in yet. Nevertheless, for this next portion of the session we need to move on to discuss how to invest the money in your College Fund."

"Hang on a minute," interrupted one woman. "We haven't talked about putting money into the College Fund yet. All we've discussed is how to set the College Fund Target. Don't we need to contribute money to the College Fund before we worry about investing it?"

"I understand why you'd ask that," said the instructor. "We did approach short-term objectives in that order, remember? First you set the Auto Fund Target or the Home Fund Target, next you determined how much you could afford to contribute per month, and with that information you calculated how long it would take you to achieve your goal. Only at that point did we discuss the investment strategy.

"For long-term objectives we need a slightly different approach. For short-term investments, the short Time Horizon and the 100% fixed income investment strategy combine to produce negligible investment growth. Therefore, you can ignore investment results when determining the required contribution and length of time to achieve the goal. Investment results don't change the contributions you must make to short term funds.

Assessing long-term objectives requires an extra step because you expect to achieve substantial investment returns which reduce your need to make contributions to the fund. We need to estimate those investment returns before we can calculate your necessary contribution."

"I think that makes sense," said the woman, a bit uneasily.

"Don't worry, it will make more sense as we do it," assured the instructor. "Think back to last week when we discussed investing your short-term Funds. The first question you must ask yourself when assessing how to invest your money is 'what is my Time Horizon?' That question was fairly simple for your short-term Funds. It is trickier for your College Fund."

"It doesn't seem so tricky," said Joe. "Isn't it eighteen years? That's the length of time between when your child is born and when they go to college."

"It's not eighteen years for me," said Mitchell. "I wish I had started saving when my children were born, but I didn't start until my older child was about eight and my younger was seven. It's either ten or eleven for me, depending on which child you use."

"Why do you use the child's first year of college?" asked Andrea. "You will be paying for college over four years, so shouldn't you use the last year of college as the end of the Time Horizon?"

At this point, everyone seemed a bit unsure, so the instructor stepped in: "You have touched on the two complications that make determining the Time Horizon for your College Fund confusing: multiple children and the extended period over which you pay for college. For a family with two or three children spread out in age, they could pay for college over a period of ten years or more. We will need to consider this range of Time Horizons as we develop an appropriate investment strategy.

"Let's return to Mitchell's situation, as it presents a relatively simple case. Mitchell has one child beginning school in one year, and another beginning school the year after that. First, as of today, what is his range of Time Horizons?"

"One year on the low end, and six years on the high end," proposed Andrea.

"Exactly. His Time Horizons span 1-6 years. We have looked at Time Horizons of this length before, when we considered Auto Funds and Home Funds, right? Do you remember our conclusions about investment strategies for this range of Time Horizons?"

A number of people called out the answer: "You shouldn't invest in equities when your Time Horizon is that short."

"Very good. Mitchell, who has a College Fund Target of $115,000, and who hopefully has the bulk of that accumulated already, should have his College Fund invested entirely in fixed income securities right now. He can't afford the risk of a drop in the stock market that would reduce the value of the savings he has accumulated."

Mitchell looked pleased. "You know how I feel about stocks," he said, "I haven't owned any in years."

"If you are all with me," said the instructor, "let's now return to Andrea's situation. Her investment strategy is less obvious. Andrea, can we use you as our example for a few minutes?"

"Sure," said Andrea.

"Good. You have a ten-year old, right?"

"Yes."

"Then your Time Horizon for your College Fund right now is 8-12 years. Remember, everyone, Mitchell's Time Horizon was 1-6 years, because his son will be starting college next year, but college is paid over the four years, not all at once. Andrea, whose daughter will start college in eight years, has a Time Horizon of 8-12 years. Is that clear to everyone?"

No one said otherwise, so he continued: "Eight to twelve years is roughly the range of Time Horizons when you can begin investing in equities. When we discussed the Home Fund, we agreed that, for a seven year Time Horizon, holding equities did little to accelerate your home purchase, because you would need to switch to fixed income investments before your equities had enough time to appreciate. The assessment is a little different as the Time Horizon lengthens to 8-12 years."

"Does it matter that the Time Horizon is a range?" asked Bruce. "I know that the fact that it is longer matters, but does it also matter that it is a range of years, instead of a single year?"

"Why would it matter?" asked Sally.

"If your stocks are down," Bruce answered, "you don't need to sell them all at once like you would have to if you were using your savings to buy a home. You only have to sell a little bit each year over four years. You have a better chance that your stocks recover."

Mitchell didn't accept that argument. "Even with more time to recover, does that mean you should take the risk? Wouldn't Andrea be better off with fixed income investments so she wouldn't need to worry about a market crash?"

"A falling stock market is not the only risk," countered Bruce. "Over eight to 12 years, inflation could drive up the cost of college insanely. Andrea's fixed income investments won't grow enough to pay for college, and she'll have to contribute more and more to her fund each year. I thought last week's discussion made it clear that for long Time Horizons, equity investments were preferable to fixed income investments."

"Wait a second," said Sally to the instructor. "Didn't you say that the financial aid formulas are based on what people can afford, not what college costs? So if college prices went up, Andrea would just get more aid, she wouldn't have to pay more, right?"

"Yes," said Bruce, before the instructor could answer. "But he also said that if we have high inflation her salary will rise, too. The EFC formula will demand that she pay more."

"Is that right?" asked Sally.

"It could happen," said the instructor. "Andrea has a little better protection against inflation than someone who does not expect financial aid, but she still has some risk. On an inflation-adjusted basis, equities grow more than fixed income investments about 80% of the time over a ten-year period and 70% of the time over a five-year period. If you have eight to 12 years, the odds are pretty good equities are going to help you. The range of Time Horizons also helps you escape the paradox that plagued your Home Fund, too. If the market falls precipitously right before your child begins college, you won't need to sell all your stocks at once. All things considered, Bruce is right: an all fixed income strategy would not be your best choice."

"So are you saying I should have all equity investments or a mixture of equity and fixed income investments in my College Fund?" asked Andrea.

"I'd suggest a mixture, at least for the next two or three years."

"In what proportion? Should it be 50/50, or weighted to one side?"

The instructor thought for a moment. "Let me hold off on answering that question. I think if we look at one more example, you will all come to a similar conclusion on your own. Jack and Isabel, can we use you again?"

"Sure," said Isabel, happy to be selected. She felt that the discussion of Investing had helped them, and she hoped for the same benefit discussing her College Fund.

"Good. Let's make sure we've got the facts. How many children do you have?"

"We have two. The older one is seven and the younger is two."

"Okay, your Time Horizon ranges from 11-20 years. What we need to know is your gross income."

"Our gross income is about $200,000," answered Jack.

A number of envious heads turned toward Jack. While he and Isabel didn't have the highest income in the class, they were close. Many of their classmates appeared surprised that a young couple with an apparently 'high' income would still have substantial financial concerns.

The instructor spoke frankly. "With an income level that high, and with children who will not overlap at college, you should not expect to receive financial aid. Your College Fund needs to carry the full load."

"How much is that?" asked Isabel nervously.

"For your seven year-old, who has eleven years before starting college, multiply 1.02^{11} x $38,000. That equals about $47,000. Over four years, you will need $188,000.[11] Your second child will require even more, as that child begins school in sixteen years. Multiply 1.02^{16} x $38,000 to get about $52,000. Multiply that by four, and your second child will cost a total of $208,000. Add them together to produce your College Fund Target, which is $396,000.

"That's a huge amount of money," said Jack.

"It sure is," agreed the instructor. "The good news is you have a lot of time - time to invest your money in equities."

"Hang on a minute," said Isabel. "Last week you told us that it was fine that we had sold our equities. Now you're going to tell us the opposite?"

"Last week we discussed your Auto Fund," answered the instructor. "Now we are discussing your College Fund. With a Time Horizon of 11 to 20 years and the distinct likelihood that you

---

[11] In truth, continued inflation while the child is in college makes the number slightly higher. The difference is immaterial in the context of the overall college savings plan.

will not receive financial aid, which puts you severely at risk for college cost inflation, you need an equity-dominated College Fund."

The instructor turned to the class. "Let's compare Jack and Isabel's situation with Andrea's. Jack and Isabel have a longer Time Horizon, 11 to 20 years instead of eight to 12. Over a twenty-year period, equities will grow more than fixed income more than 90% of the time. Jack and Isabel's longer Time Horizon allows for a much greater weighting of equities than Andrea's Time Horizon allows. Also, Jack and Isabel need to fear inflation much more than Andrea. Not only do they have a longer Time Horizon, giving inflation more time to erode the value of their savings, they do not have the inflation-cushion that financial aid will likely provide Andrea."

"This all makes sense," said one man. "But it doesn't tell us what to do. What proportion of equities should they each use?"

The instructor turned to the flip chart. "When your children are young, you want the money in their College Funds invested in equities. By the time they near college age, you want the money invested in fixed income. Therefore, you need to transition your College Fund investments from equities to fixed income as your children age. Here is a chart showing the Recommended College Fund Asset Allocation:

Table 13-1
Recommended College Fund Asset Allocation

Child' Age	Percentage Of Equities in College Fund
0 – 7	100%
8 – 9	80%
10 – 11	60%
12 – 13	40%
14 – 15	20%
16 and over	0%

The students looked at the chart and intuitively felt it made sense. Therefore, they were surprised by the instructor's next comment: "Unfortunately, if I told you to simply follow the transition recommended in this chart, I would be giving you very bad advice. Does anyone recognize the potential flaw in following this transition?"

No one answered.

"I'll give you a hint. It has to do with Time Horizons," the instructor offered.

After a few more moments, Joe thought he saw the problem: "It's the same problem we had with the Home Fund. If you need to begin selling your equities well before the end of your Time Horizon, your Time Horizon isn't as long as it seems."

"Very good, Joe," said the instructor. "If I tell you that when your child turns eight, you must sell 20% of the equities in your College Fund, I have effectively shortened your Time Horizon for that portion of your College Fund. In that case, you should never have invested that portion of your College Fund in equities, as the Time Horizon wasn't long enough."

"I don't understand," said one woman. "Should we follow this chart or not?"

She was not alone. Everyone was confused by the turn the discussion had taken.

The instructor sympathized with them. "Most of the time, you should follow the Recommended College Fund Asset Allocation. Following it will allow you to benefit substantially from the higher returns and inflation protection equity investing offers. At the same time, you cannot follow it inflexibly. The advantage of a long Time Horizon is that you do not have to sell your equities when their value has fallen. You can wait for them to recover. You don't want to eliminate the advantage of a long Time Horizon by slavishly following the recommended asset allocation."

The class began to understand, though plenty of questions remained. Andrea asked, "How do we decide if the equities are down?"

"Since you will be investing in index funds, it won't be difficult. Just compare the rate of return on the S&P 500 to the rate of inflation, beginning at the time you began contributing to your College Fund.[12] If the rate of return is lower than the rate of inflation, your equity investment is probably down."

"And what do we do if our equity investment is down?" Andrea followed up.

"Nothing. Don't re-allocate the investments your College Fund, even if the chart says it is time to do so. Wait until the rate of return on the S&P 500 has caught up with the inflation rate. When that happens, you can re-allocate to the ratio suggested in the Recommended College Fund Asset Allocation."

He turned a page on the flip chart and wrote:

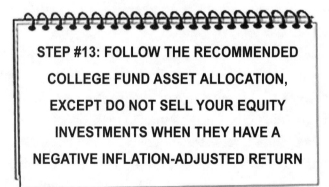

STEP #13: FOLLOW THE RECOMMENDED COLLEGE FUND ASSET ALLOCATION, EXCEPT DO NOT SELL YOUR EQUITY INVESTMENTS WHEN THEY HAVE A NEGATIVE INFLATION-ADJUSTED RETURN

Mitchell wasn't satisfied with that answer. "What if the rate of return on the S&P 500 never catches up to the inflation rate?" asked Mitchell.

---

[12] For a table showing the after-inflation return on the S&P 500 for historical periods back through 1950, go to www.dougwarshauer.com

"In that case, you would still be holding all your equities when your child reaches college age," the instructor answered.

Not surprisingly, at least a few people were startled by the response. They started to speak, but the instructor cut them off. He said, "I know this sounds contrary to what I've told you already. It isn't. If you begin contributing to your College Fund while your child is young, the chances that the rate of return on equities remains below inflation until the child reaches college age is small. It's not impossible, but quite small. On the other hand, it is extremely likely that you will have benefited by holding equity investments rather than fixed income investments during this period. Again, it isn't certain, but extremely likely.

"Although it seems quite contrary to my earlier message, that you don't want to be holding equity investments immediately prior to the end of your Time Horizon, the fact is that benefiting from your long initial Time Horizon requires that, under certain unusual circumstances, you would continue to hold equities until the beginning of college."

Mitchell pressed his case. "Isn't it possible that you would be holding equities right before college, and then they would drop substantially in value, and you would have even less money in your fund than you did before, and no time to make it up?"

"It is possible," the instructor conceded. "Unfortunately, there are no guarantees when it comes to your financial planning. You can only do your best to minimize risks. The risk of equities generating a lower return than inflation for 20 years, then experiencing a severe decline without a quick recovery, is theoretically possible but, according to history, highly improbable. You cannot avoid that risk without subjecting yourself to a far greater risk by avoiding equity investments entirely and exposing yourself to the potential that an extended period of high inflation will reduce the value of your fixed income investments."

Mitchell, whose good nature made him one of the most likeable members of the seminar, chuckled and said, "You're a tough guy to argue against. You may be right, but I've got to say I'm glad my kids are old enough that I don't have to buy any equities anyway."

Sally raised her hand. "I've got one more question. Since my kids are three years apart, how do I decide my equity allocation? Do I take the average of the two kids?"

"Sure," the instructor answered. "If you should be at 40% equities for one child and 20% for the other, it's fine to be at 30% overall. Or you could keep separate funds for each child.

"Let's take our break now. We are just about ready to put it all together. By combining the College Fund Target with this basic investment strategy and our assumptions about the rates of return of equity and fixed income investments, we can determine how much of your net income you will need to contribute each year to the College Fund."

"I'm not sure I follow you," said one man.

"Remember that at the beginning of today's session I told you that everyone would leave here knowing how to determine the amount of money that they must save each year to ensure an adequate College Fund?" asked the instructor. "That amount will be a percentage of your net income. When we come back, I will show you exactly how you calculate that percentage."

CHAPTER FOURTEEN

Setting an Annual Savings Rate

It didn't take long for everyone to return from the break. They knew that the entire college savings program would come together in the final part of the session. Each participant hoped that, within minutes, he would learn the amount he would need to save each year for college. Even more, each participant hoped, perhaps prayed, for a low number.

The instructor initiated the discussion with a brief review: "We began today by listing the four main sources of uncertainty that make saving for college difficult. You now know how to deal with each of those. You can all set a College Fund Target, an amount that will enable you to pay for your children's college education. You also know how to invest the money in your College Fund so that you maximize the likelihood that you will achieve your target.

"All that remains is setting an annual savings rate. Once you know the percentage of your net income that you should contribute each year to your College Fund, you will know everything you need to know."

"Is the savings rate the same for everyone?" asked one man.

"What do you all think?" responded the instructor. "Based on what you have learned so far, do you think everyone can use the same savings rate?"

"I don't think so," said Joe. "People with lower incomes probably can have low savings rates. After all, you said that people with incomes below $30,000 don't need to save at all."

"I'm not sure they can have low savings rates," disputed Bruce. "They might be saving less money in absolute dollars but not as a percentage of their income. Actually, I think people with high incomes can have low savings rate. After all, if you earn as much as Bill Gates, you don't need to save much of your income to pay for college."

As usual, when two participants made equally persuasive arguments that appeared contradictory, the class looked to the instructor for clarity. "You are both right," he said. "People with lower incomes can normally have low college savings rates, as financial aid covers the bulk of their college costs. Also, people with very high incomes can also have low college savings rates, as the cost of college impacts them relatively less than people with moderately high incomes who don't qualify for much or any financial aid.

"People in the middle get squeezed. Families with net incomes between $80,000 and $140,000 tend to need to save the highest percentage of their net income for college. As a family's net income either falls below $80,000 or grows above $140,000, the percentage of its net income that it must save for college diminishes."

"That's just typical. The middle class always takes it on the chin," said one woman unhappily.

"It doesn't seem fair," agreed another man.

"Fair or not," said the instructor, "that's the way it is. You don't have to like it, but you do have to recognize it. You now know that everyone does not need to save at the same rate, and that one factor that affects how much you need to save each year is your income. There is another important factor. Can anyone guess what it is?"

"The age of your children?" suggested Sally.

"That's right," said the instructor. "The younger your children are when you begin to contribute to their College Fund, the lower your annual savings rate. This should be intuitively obvious. By beginning to make your contributions when your children are young, you allow yourself more years over which to spread your contributions, and you provide your investments more time to grow."

Mark couldn't help himself. "That's what I've been trying to say all along. You have been insisting that we not contribute money to our long-term objectives and that instead we pay off debt and buy a car and a house. I kept trying to say if you do all that it will be too late to save for the long-term objectives. Now, finally, you are agreeing with me: you need to contribute to your kids' College Fund when they are young and not wait until they are about to graduate from high school!"

The class listened sympathetically to Mark. Many of them shared similar thoughts. They waited for the instructor's response.

"It does sound like I'm trying to have it both ways, doesn't it?" agreed the instructor. "I'm not. You still must do the other things first. You must pay off your debt. You must pay cash for your cars so that you do not take on new debt to buy a car. Although it is very advantageous to begin saving for the College Fund when your children are young, it is not at all advantageous to contribute to a College Fund at the same time you have high-interest rate consumer debt compounding.

"The simple, inescapable fact is that the interest will accumulate on your debt faster than the value of your College Fund will grow. Money that you otherwise would have been able to contribute to your College Fund in the future will be squandered by debt payments. Ultimately, you will have more difficulty reaching your College Fund Target than had you first eliminated your debt and only then began to contribute to the College Fund."

"I see your point," said Sally, "but I don't know what to do about it. If we follow this plan, our children will be nearly college age before we're ready to begin contributing to the College Fund. What do we do?"

"Beginning to contribute to your College Fund later is not as good as beginning to contribute when your children are young," specified the instructor, "but it's not necessarily a disaster. You simply need a larger College Fund contribution when you do begin to contribute. As this session progresses, you'll see that while the benefit of early saving is obvious, even a family who begins saving in high school has a range of alternatives.

"We're jumping ahead. Before we can get to that, you all need to learn how to calculate your College Fund savings rate."

He turned to the flip chart and wrote:

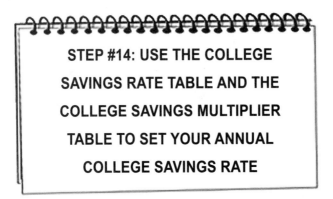

STEP #14: USE THE COLLEGE
SAVINGS RATE TABLE AND THE
COLLEGE SAVINGS MULTIPLIER
TABLE TO SET YOUR ANNUAL
COLLEGE SAVINGS RATE

"What are the College Savings Rate Table and the College Savings Multiplier Tables?" asked a number of people in unison.

"They are tools that will help you set your savings rate," the instructor answered. "I think you'll find them surprisingly easy to use, once you get familiar with them. To show you how to use these tools, let's work through some examples.

"We'll start with the ideal situation, someone who begins saving when their child is born. Joe, as you are the youngest one here, let's use you for this example. You're not married, no kids, right?"

"Right," said Joe, thinking the idea of marriage and children was far off.

"Joe is lucky to be here now. Let's assume he follows through on what we've discussed in this seminar. He pays off all his debt, he contributes to his Auto Fund, and he pays cash for his car. Perhaps he even has begun to contribute to his Home Fund by the time he has a child. As soon as his child is born, he can begin contributing to a College Fund. Let's do the math to calculate what percentage of his net income he must contribute each year.

"Suppose Joe's gross income, by the time his child is born, has grown to $70,000. Assuming 3% merit increases for the following 18 years, his income when the child is college age will be $119,000. His EFC will be approximately $28,000. His College Fund Target will be $112,000. You should all be with me so far, as we have done similar computations for Andrea and Mitchell already. Any questions?"

There were none, so he continued. "Joe has about 21 years before his child finishes college, so he has 21 years to invest the College Fund. We need to estimate the results of those investments. First, let's assume that he follows the Recommended College Fund Asset Allocation. Next, we need to estimate the rate of return of both the equity investments and the fixed income investments. Remember, our estimated return will be in today's dollars. We want an 'after inflation' or 'real' investment return. By using a real return, we don't need to worry about what inflation will be. That removes a major source of uncertainty."

"Even without worrying about inflation, I think trying to predict your investment return over 21 years is nothing but a wild guess," interrupted Mitchell. "You could be way, way off."

"That's true," admitted the instructor. "But we need to make the best guess we can. Fortunately, Joe has 21 years, so he can make corrections along the way if necessary."

"That reminds me of what you said about our income," pointed out Andrea. "If our income grows faster or slower than expected, we modify our plan. We can do the same thing if our investments grow faster or slower than expected, right?"

"That's right. But we need a starting point. Last week, when we discussed equity investing, we agreed that you could expect to earn 6.5% per year by using index funds. For your fixed income investments, an annual return of about 1% per year would be reasonable. Using those assumptions, it's not hard to calculate how much money a person must save each year, depending upon the age of the child at the time they begin this savings program."

The instructor turned a page on the flip chart revealing a table, then turned back to the class.

"This chart shows, for every $1,000 a family ultimately needs to accumulate, how much they must contribute in the first year they begin their savings program. As you can see, the older the child, the larger the amount the family must contribute."

TABLE 7-1

COLLEGE SAVINGS RATE TABLE

Child's Current Age	Current Required Contribution per $1,000 of College Fund Target
1	$27
2	29
3	32
4	35
5	39
6	43
7	47
8	53
9	58
10	65
11	73
12	83
13	94
14	109
15	127
16	152
17	186
18	237

"Let's do the math and see how this would work for Joe. His College Fund Target is $112,000. Since he will begin when his child is born, he will only need to contribute $27 that year for every $1,000 of his College Fund Target. To calculate his contribution, multiply $27 by $112,000 and divide by 1,000. He will need to contribute $3,024."

"Does he contribute the same amount each year?" asked one woman.

"No," answered the instructor. "He must contribute the same *percentage of his income* each year. As his income increases, his contributions must increase with it. With $70,000 of gross income, he will have approximately $49,000 of net income.[13] By dividing $3,024 by $49,000, we can calculate that he must contribute 6.1% of his net income to his College Fund."

"And he has to continue to contribute 6.1% of his net income each year?" confirmed the woman.

"Exactly," said the instructor.

LET'S DO THE MATH

College Fund Target	$112,000
Age of Child	1
Contribution Required per $1,000	$27
(from Table 7-1)	
Current Year Contribution	$3,024
(112,000 x 27 ÷ 1,000)	
Gross Income	$70,000
Net Income Multiplier	.7
(from Appendix 2)	
Net Income	$49,000
Savings Rate as Percent of Net Income	**6.1%**

---

[13] A chart showing the recommended percentage to use to convert gross income to net income is included in Appendix 2.

"If I understand this correctly, assuming my gross income is $70,000 when my first child is born, I should start putting 6.1% of my net income into the College Fund. I continue putting 6.1% of my net income in every year, and that will be sufficient to eventually pay for college," said Joe.

"In a nutshell, yes, but you need to be prepared to make adjustments along the way. If your income grows faster than 3% over inflation, you'll need to boost your savings. Or, if your equities do much worse than 6.5% per year over inflation, you may need to boost your savings. Remember Step #11: you must periodically recalculate your College Savings Plan."

"Do you have to adjust your savings rate each year according to how your stocks do? If so, you'd be constantly making changes," pointed out Bruce.

"You definitely don't want to do that. Your stocks will sometimes grow much faster than 6.5%, other times they'll fall. Unless there is a steep drop in the value of your equity investments, I wouldn't adjust your savings rate based on your equity investment performance until your child is about fourteen years old. Until then, you have little idea how they'll ultimately perform. Even if they ultimately earn less than 6.5% per year, you will still have seven years to adjust your savings to make up the shortfall."

"What if I have a second child?" asked Joe.

"That's different. You must immediately re-calculate your savings plan when you have another child."

The instructor paused for a moment. "I know this is a bit confusing. We'll do a couple more examples to help you understand. Let's go back to Andrea. We calculated Andrea's EFC to be $13,000. Her College Fund Target is $52,000. Using the College Savings Rate Table, with a single child of ten years of age, she needs to save $3,380 this year, and 7.9% of her income for the next twelve years.

"Now, let's add another wrinkle. Andrea has some money saved already, doesn't she?"

"I do," said Andrea. "I have about $10,000 saved so far."

"Andrea needs to factor in her existing savings. The College Savings Rate Table tells you the required savings rate if you are starting from scratch. Since many of you have some college savings already, you need to account for it."

He turns a page on the flip chart revealing another table, the College Savings Multiplier Table.

TABLE 7-2
COLLEGE SAVINGS MULTIPLIER TABLE

Child's Current Age	Multiplier on Existing College Savings
1	2.1
2	2.0
3	1.9
4	1.8
5	1.7
6	1.6
7	1.5
8	1.4
9	1.3
10	1.2
11	1.2
12	1.1
13	1.1
14	1.1
15 and over	1.0

"Here is how to do it," he continued. "Multiply your current savings by the appropriate multiplier, given the current age of your child. The College Savings Multiplier Table tells you what you can expect your current savings to be worth when your child reaches college age. Andrea's $10,000 savings will be worth about $12,000 when her daughter reaches college age. Subtracting that from her College Fund Target of $52,000, Andrea's future savings only needs to grow to $40,000. She needs to save $2,600 this year, and 6.1% of her net income for the next twelve years.

LET'S DO THE MATH

College Fund Target	$52,000
Current Savings	$10,000
Age of Child	10
Multiplier on Savings	1.2
(from Table 7-2)	
Future Value of Savings	$12,000
(10,000 x 1.2)	
Unfunded Target	$40,000
(52,000 – 12,000)	
Age of Child	10
Contribution Required per $1,000	$65
(from Table 7-1)	
Current Year Contribution	$2,600
(40,000 x 65 ÷ 1,000)	
Gross Income	$60,000
Net Income Multiplier	.71
(from Appendix 2)	
Net Income	$42,600
Savings Rate as Percent of Net Income	**6.1%**
($2,600 ÷ $42,600)	

"Wow! That's the same as Joe! Why isn't her savings rate much higher than his if she's starting ten years later?" Sally asked.

"Because Andrea will probably end up with a lot more financial aid than Joe. Andrea's College Fund Target is $52,000, but Joe's is

$112,000. Joe has more time, but he needs to save more than twice as much money."

The class again looked confused. The math was more complicated than in the previous sessions. The instructor recognized the challenge: "I know this is hard. Don't give up, we're almost done. Let's look at Jack and Isabel and see how it works with two children.

"Their gross income is $200,000, the older child is seven years old, and the younger is two. Because the children will not overlap at college, Jack and Isabel will not receive any financial aid. Assuming the couple is willing to pay for an average cost private school, they need to expect to spend about $47,000 per year for the older child, meaning their College Fund Target is $188,000."

He turns to Jack: "You have some savings already, don't you?"

"We do. It's the money we told you about last week, that was all in cash," said Jack.

"How much is there?"

"About $30,000."

The instructor turned to the College Savings Multiplier Table. "With a seven year old child, you can expect your current savings to increase 1.5 times by the time she reaches college. 1.5 times 30,000 equals 45,000. Subtract that 45,000 from the 188,000 College Fund Target. You need your future savings to grow to $143,000."

The instructor surveyed the class. "Is everyone with me so far?"

Everyone seemed to be, so he now turned to the College Savings Rate Table. "With a seven year old child, you need to save $47 for every $1,000 you need to ultimately accumulate. Multiply 47 times 135,000 and divide by 1,000. You need to save $6,721 this year. Assuming your net income is about $130,000, you'll need to save 5.2% of your net income."

"That's just for the older child, right?" asked Isabel.

"Yes," the instructor responded. "Now let's consider the second child. For a two year old, you have a higher College Fund Target, because we expect college prices to continue to rise faster than inflation, and you have another five years before college begins. Your College Fund Target for the younger child is $208,000."

"And you counted all our savings already," said Isabel, painfully.

"The good news is, you are beginning to save very early for the second child. According to the College Savings Rate Table, you only need to save $29 for every $1,000 you need to ultimately accumulate. Multiply 29 times 200,000 and divide by 1,000. You need to save $6,032 this year. Again, assuming your net income is about $130,000, you'll need to save 4.6% of your net income."

"To determine our total savings, we should add the two children together, right?" Jack asked.

"Right. By the way, if you had split your existing savings equally between the two children, the total amount you will need to save in the future wouldn't change."

Jack quickly added the numbers, then looked up: "That means we need to save $12,753, which is 9.8% of our income."

LET'S DO THE MATH

Child 1

College Fund Target	$188,000
Current Savings	$30,000
Age of Child	7
Multiplier on Savings	1.5
(from Table 7-2)	
Future Value of Savings	$45,000
(30,000 x 1.5)	
Unfunded Target	$143,000
(188,000 – 45,000)	
Age of Child	7
Contribution Required per $1,000	$47
(from Table 7-1)	
Current Year Contribution	$6,721
(143,000 x 47 ÷ 1,000)	
Gross Income	$200,000
Net Income Multiplier	.65
(from Appendix 2)	
Net Income	$130,000
Savings Rate as Percent of Net Income	**5.2%**
($6,721 ÷ $130,000)	

Continued

LET'S DO THE MATH

Child 2

College Fund Target	$208,000
Current Savings	$0
Age of Child	2
Multiplier on Savings	1.5
(from Table 7-2)	
Future Value of Savings	$0
(0 x 1.5)	
Unfunded Target	$208,000
(208,000 – 0)	
Age of Child	2
Contribution Required per $1,000	$29
(from Table 7-1)	
Current Year Contribution	$6,032
(208,000 x 29 ÷ 1,000)	
Gross Income	$200,000
Net Income Multiplier	.65
Net Income	$130,000
Savings Rate as Percent of Net Income	4.6%
($6,032 ÷ $130,000)	
Combined Current Year Contribution	$12,753
Combined Savings Rate as Percent of Net Income	**9.8%**
(5.2% + 4.6%)	

"If we save 10% of our net income every year, like you told us to a few weeks ago, nearly everything must go to saving for college?" asked Isabel painfully.

"For the next twenty years, yes," agreed the instructor, sympathetically. "And that assumes your equity investments earn a real rate of return of 6.5% per year. You can't afford to lose money like you have been."

"That's pretty scary," complained Jack. "You told us we'd feel good about this class, but I'm not feeling too good right now."

"Maybe not, but you may feel better later, when this sinks in. You'll know what you need to do. You now know how to effectively invest your equities. You are good savers, so you can be confident that you have a plan that will meet your children's needs.

"Before we wrap up for the day, let's look at Mitchell. Remember, Mitchell's older son will begin college next year, and his younger son will begin the year after that. Instead of considering the children separately, it is easier to calculate Mitchell's savings needs by for both children at once, because they will overlap in college by three years. We already have calculated that Mitchell's College Fund Target for the two children combined is $115,000."

"Can I try to work through the math myself?" Mitchell asked.

"Sure, go ahead," the instructor responded, pleased to see Mitchell take the initiative.

"I've got $80,000 saved so far," Mitchell began. "According to the College Savings Multiplier Table, that isn't going to grow in the next year. So I just subtract the $80,000 from the $115,000 College Fund Target, right?"

"That's right," said the instructor. "Since you need to be in fixed income investments at this point – which I know is fine with you, Mitchell – you can't expect any material investment growth in the next year."

Mitchell smiled along with the rest of the class. "So I need enough additional savings to reach $35,000. Since my son is 17, according to the College Savings Rate Table, I have to save $186 for every $1,000. To calculate the amount I need to save, I multiply 186 times 35,000 and divide by 1,000, right?"

"Very good," said the instructor. "What do you get?"

Mitchell punched the numbers on his calculator. "$6,510," he said.

"And what percent is that of your net income?"

Mitchell punched in a few more numbers. "Eight percent," he answered. "That's what I need to save to send the boys to private schools, isn't it?"

"Yes. If you limited them to public schools, remember, your College Fund Target dropped to about $101,000. You'd only need an additional $21,000. To reach that, you would only need to save about 4.8% of your net income."

LET'S DO THE MATH

Private Schools

College Fund Target	$115,000
Current Savings	$80,000
Age of Child	17
Multiplier on Savings	1.0
(from Table 7-2)	
Future Value of Savings	$80,000
(80,000 x 1.0)	
Unfunded Target	$35,000
(115,000 – 80,000)	
Age of Child	17
Contribution Required per $1,000	$186
(from Table 7-1)	
Current Year Contribution	$6,510
(35,000 x 186 ÷ 1,000)	
Gross Income	$120,000
Net Income Multiplier	.68
(from Appendix 2)	
Net Income	$81,600
Savings Rate as Percent of Net Income	**8.0%**
($6,510 ÷ $81,000)	

Public Schools

College Fund Target	$101,000
Current Savings	$80,000
Age of Child	17
Multiplier on Savings	1.0
(from Table 7-2)	
Future Value of Savings	$80,000
(80,000 x 1.0)	
Unfunded Target	$21,000
(115,000 – 80,000)	
Age of Child	17
Contribution Required per $1,000	$186
(from Table 7-1)	
Current Year Contribution	$3,906
(21,000 x 186 ÷ 1,000)	
Gross Income	$120,000
Net Income Multiplier	.68
(from Appendix 2)	
Net Income	$81,600
Savings Rate as Percent of Net Income	**4.8%**
($3,906 ÷ $81,000)	

"That's all the difference is? 8.0% vs. 4.8%? That's only three percent a year. I might as well let them go to private schools."

"I have to admit that I'm shocked," said Sally. "This is not intuitive at all. I would have thought, especially for someone with an income like Mitchell's, where his children went to school would make a much bigger difference."

"You're right, it isn't very intuitive. For Mitchell, it turns out that the three years the boys will both be in school makes a major difference. If they didn't overlap, private schools would matter more. Of course, if they didn't overlap, he'd have more years of potential savings left, too.

"Mitchell's case is a good lesson. You need to do the calculations to determine what you need to save. It's very hard to guess without doing the calculations. Once you have done the calculations, you can make an informed choice, balancing the additional savings required to allow your children to attend private schools against the benefits those schools provide."

Eric looked like something was bothering him. "Mitchell is lucky, or, let me rephrase that, Mitchell is benefiting from having proactively saved $80,000 already. I just calculated what he'd have to save starting now if he hadn't already saved $80,000. He would need to save 26% of his income per year. That could be where Sally and I end up. By the time we can start saving for college, we'll need to save 26% of our net income per year. What if we can't do that?"

"That's a great question, Eric," said the instructor. "What do you all think? If Eric and Sally need to save 26% of their net income, and they can't do it, what could they do?"

No one seemed sure. The instructor waited for someone to answer. "Who can answer Eric's question? Think of it this way: suppose Mitchell hadn't saved the $80,000. What could he do if he couldn't save 26% of his income for the next six years?"

"He could limit them to in-state public schools," said Jack. "That would help a little."

"Yes," agreed the instructor, "we know that would save $14,000. That's not enough to replace $80,000 in savings, but a start. What else could he do?"

"He could insist that his kids work during school and over the summers to make up the difference," proposed Bruce.

"He could do that, but his children's income would reduce his financial aid substantially. Even if the children could generate $20,000 after netting out the impact on financial aid, Mitchell would still have a shortfall. What can he do?"

"Could he borrow the money?" asked Joe unsurely, thinking that the idea of borrowing has been taboo in this course.

"Yes!" exclaimed the instructor. "He can borrow the money! You probably all have the impression that I think there is no place for debt, but that's not entirely true. In the circumstance where you have waited too long to save adequately for college, you may have no choice but to take out some debt."

"I don't get it," said Mark. "If it's so important that we not be in debt before college, why is it okay to go into debt to pay for college?"

Mark was not the only one puzzled by that seeming contradiction. "It's pretty simple," answered the instructor. "First, the debt you have before your children start college is probably the worst kind of debt: credit card or consumer debt. The debt you will use to pay for college should be less counterproductive. Hopefully, by the time your children reach college, you will have built up enough equity in your home that you can use a home equity line or second mortgage to fund your college expenses. The lower interest rate and tax deductibility of this debt makes it less disadvantageous.

"If you don't have the capacity to borrow against your home, you can take advantage of the U.S. Department of Education's PLUS – Parent Loans for Undergraduate Students – program. Those loans, though much less attractive than a home equity loan, still present a better alternative than credit card loans. You will be eligible for a PLUS loan as long as you have reasonable credit, which you will certainly have if you have been following this overall program.

"Also, waiting until the children reach college allows you to limit your debt to the minimum necessary to bridge the gap between your College Fund and the actual costs of college. Suppose instead that you allowed your credit card balances to remain outstanding and grow while you aggressively contributed to your College Fund, hoping to ensure you have enough money in the fund to pay for a private school education. Then, if your child, somewhat ironically, chooses an in-state school, you have far more money than necessary in the College Fund, and you will have built up and paid years and years of interest on credit card debt for no reason."

"So you're saying that you can use debt as a last resort to help pay for college, if it turns out that your College Fund comes up short," suggested Sally.

"That's right. Knowing that you have that possibility as a last resort should give you comfort along the way. Let's summarize what we've learned. As soon as you are debt free and have adequately taken care of your short-term objectives, you want to begin contributing to your College Fund. The sooner you begin, the lower the annual savings rate. You all now know how to determine the savings rate you'll need.

"Invest the money in your College Fund according to the Recommended College Fund Asset Allocation.

"Recalculate your required savings periodically, especially if your earnings grow more than three percent a year faster than inflation or if your stocks fall substantially.

"Finally, if you cannot save the required amount, save as much as you can. Take comfort that you will almost certainly be able to borrow enough money to make up whatever shortfall you face."

The expressions on the faces of the group reflected both supreme tiredness and the satisfaction that they had learned everything they hoped to learn. They knew that, upon leaving the seminar that night, they would never think the same way about saving for college. They would feel the power of their knowledge, and they would sleep better for it.

Though everyone seemed ready to leave, a woman asked one final question: "Suppose we do have to borrow money to pay for college? What will we use to pay it back?"

"Once people have reached the point in their life when their children are out of college," answered the instructor, "they normally have only one major savings objective remaining, retirement. If your College Fund proves sufficient to pay for college, you will begin to devote all your subsequent savings to your Retirement Fund. If you need to use your post-college savings to pay down college debt, you will defer your ability to save for retirement.

"You can all keep that thought in your minds for the next week. When we reconvene here next week, saving for retirement will be our subject."

Save for Retirement

CHAPTER FIFTEEN

What You Need for Retirement

O n the final day of the seminar, nearly all the participants arrived early. They had grown close to each other over the past five weeks, and they sought to make the most of the opportunity to chat with their new friends one last time. The frank and open classroom discussions had helped them bond and develop a closeness that they were reluctant to see end. Even Joe, whose youthfulness had made him feel an outsider on the first day, had come to see many of his compatriots as real friends.

The pre-class discussion, which the prior week had a mirthful color due to Mitchell's amusing story of his son's college tour, had a more bittersweet tone this time. Partly it came from the sadness of finality, but a touch of hopeless resignation regarding today's subject, retirement, also infected the conversation. In Eric's words, "It seems strange to worry about retirement at 30 years old, but Sally and I both have the feeling that retirement won't be an option when the time comes. After what we've learned the last four weeks, we can't even begin saving for retirement for the next twenty years. I hope we stay healthy enough to keep working forever."

"At my age, it's not strange at all to worry about it, but the picture's no prettier," answered Mitchell. "After last week, you all know that most of my savings will be going toward college for the next six years. By that time, I'll be 61. It's a good thing I like to work, because I'm going to be doing it for a while."

"You are lucky you like to work," Andrea said. "I would quit my job today if I could. But I honestly don't think about retirement. It's too far off in the distance, and I've got more immediate problems. I hope there is still Social Security when my time comes, because that's about the only hope I have of retiring."

"I wouldn't count on that," said Joe. "I've read that Social Security is going to be bankrupt in thirty years. I'm sure I'll never see a penny from it."

At that moment, the instructor came rushing through the door. He was a few minutes late, and very apologetic: "Hello everyone. I'm sorry to keep you all waiting, especially today when we have so much ground to cover. In this session, we will collect the various strands of thought and weave them into a coherent whole, so that you understand not only how to save for retirement, but how all the financial decisions over the course of your life combine to achieve all your objectives. Let's get right into it."

The instructor quickly settled himself into his seat. The others, though a bit reluctant to so quickly abandon their conversation, did the same. The instructor began. "Even more than saving for college, saving for retirement can seem overwhelming. It will help to begin our discussion by teasing out some of the specific challenges involved in saving for retirement. Everyone, feel free to speak up: what makes saving for retirement so uncertain?"

Mitchell spoke first this time. "My number one fear is outliving my savings. I might have enough money to retire and live well for a few years, but soon I'll start worrying the money's going to run out. At some point, you can't go back to work. If you're out of savings, you're out of luck. If I knew my wife and I would live until age 80, and then we'd be gone, we could determine what we need and we'd be alright. But life doesn't work that way, does it?"

"It's even worse," added Bruce. "Even knowing the exact date of your death, you couldn't be sure you have enough savings. You don't know what things will cost years after you retire. Mitchell said that if he knew he and his wife would die at age 80, he could calculate what they need to retire. I question that. If he retires at age 65, he'd have fifteen years of inflation eroding the value of his savings. With high inflation, he could run out of money even without living past age 80."

Joe seemed eager to add to that thought. "If that's a problem for Mitchell, think about what it's like for someone like me. He has fifteen years of inflation, I might have sixty! Do you imagine people in 1950 had an idea what things would cost today? It's impossible to know how much money I'll need when I retire. I have been surprised a number of times in this class, but I'll be especially surprised today if anyone can show me how to calculate how much money I need to save for retirement."

"I think you might be surprised," said the instructor confidently. "Any other issues?" No one responded. "What about Social Security? Aren't any of you concerned about Social Security?"

"I don't think any of us are counting on Social Security," answered Mark flatly. "If we get it, great, but I don't expect anything."

"I'm counting on it," said Andrea. "I'm going to need it. There's no way I can save enough without Social Security. I'd be working forever."

"Okay," said the instructor, standing up and walking to the flip chart. "You have already touched on many of the uncertainties inherent in saving for retirement. We can approach your Retirement Fund like we did your College Fund. First, I will list the three key questions you must address to evaluate your retirement savings needs. We will discuss each question, and I will show you all how you can answer those questions sufficiently to develop a Retirement Fund Target. Once you have a Retirement Fund Target, you can establish a savings plan that will enable you to meet that Target. Here are the three questions."

QUESTIONS IMPACTING SAVING FOR RETIREMENT

- How much will you spend each year you are retired?

- How long will you be retired?

- How much income will you receive from Social Security?

The instructor sat down and continued. "The first two questions cover expenses, the amount of money you will spend during your retirement. The last question addresses the amount of income you will have to support those expenses. If you can estimate the amounts for each of those three questions, you can calculate the difference between your retirement expenses and your retirement income. To retire, you will need sufficient savings in your Retirement Fund to cover that difference."

The class looked a little skeptical. Despite all they had learned over the course of the seminar, they still didn't accept anything unquestioningly. Jack appeared to speak for everyone when he commented, "You make it sound simple, but those are three tough questions. It's impossible to answer them accurately."

"It's not impossible, but it is complex," the instructor contended. "We will analyze each question, and you will learn how to answer each with a surprising degree of confidence.

"Begin with the first question -- how much you will spend each year of your retirement. As Bruce and Joe pointed out, the unpredictability of inflation makes it virtually impossible to know how much money you will need to spend when you retire. Does this problem sound familiar to any of you? Can you think of a similar issue that we have come across earlier in this seminar?"

Eric was quick to answer. "We had the same problem predicting the price of college."

"Exactly," said the instructor. "Do you remember how we handled it?"

"We ignored inflation. We forecast college cost in today's dollars, so inflation didn't matter. Does that work for retirement, too?"

"It does if you're consistent. As long as you forecast your income growth in constant dollars, using only merit increases and ignoring inflationary increases, and you forecast your investment growth in constant dollars, you can forecast your retirement expenses in constant dollars, too."

Joe was not fully convinced: "You are saying that right now, at 23 years old, I can forecast what I am going to spend in retirement? I understand the idea of constant dollars, but this seems a little far-fetched. Won't my retirement expenses depend on how much I earn during my career? If I hit it big and become a millionaire, won't I spend more than if I never progress beyond my current job?"

"Good question, Joe," said the instructor. He turned to the class. "Joe makes a good case that the amount he will spend in retirement depends upon the actual earnings growth he achieves. This should also remind you of an issue we discussed in the college savings class. Does anyone remember?"

"I do," said Andrea. "The more our earnings grew, the less financial aid we would receive, so the more we had to spend on college." She thought for a moment. "Are you saying the more our earnings grow, the more money we'll have and the more we'll spend on retirement?"

"In a sense I am. As your income grows over your lifetime, your spending will grow proportionately. In retirement, you will want to maintain the lifestyle you achieved while you were working. The more you earn while you work, the more you will expect to spend in retirement."

"But our income growth is still unpredictable," protested Joe. "That's what I meant when I said could become a millionaire or I could go nowhere."

"This may sound like splitting hairs," responded the instructor, "but it's not unpredictable, it's just hard to predict accurately. For your college fund, I suggested you estimate three percent annual merit increases. Remember how Andrea explained to us why, even if that prediction turned out wrong, it didn't matter? The same applies to retirement savings. Suppose you estimated your income would grow at three percent, and one year you get a ten percent raise. That hefty raise will eventually impact your lifestyle, so you need more savings. What do you do?"

"Save most of the big raise?" guessed Joe.

"Right! Don't adjust your spending fully upward until you have brought your savings up to the level you now need. Put the bulk of your unexpected raise into your Retirement Fund."

Eric raised the opposite question: "I think I know the answer, but if your earnings grow slower than you predicted, you end up with excess savings, right?"

"That's right," answered the instructor with satisfaction. "If you based your savings plan – and we'll discuss the details of that savings plan soon – on the expectation of three percent annual raises, and you only earn raises of two percent per year, you will have contributed enough money to your Retirement Fund to support retirement spending *greater* than the expenditures you could afford while you worked.

"I know this seems counterintuitive, but it's true. As long as you periodically modify your Retirement Plan as your circumstances change, your initial forecast does not need to be accurate for your plan to work. Using constant dollars and a three percent merit raise expectation, you can forecast the future income level which will determine your retirement spending."

"There is a piece missing," said Andrea. "To make that calculation, you would need to know when you will retire, wouldn't you? Someone who retires at age 70 would have ten more years for their income to grow than someone who retires at age 60."

"No," responded the instructor. "Assuming your income will continue to grow at three percent until you are age 70, or even age 60, would set an unrealistically high expectation for your retirement spending. Most people's income growth slows down by the time they reach their mid-fifties. Even if you are lucky enough to continue to increase your income during your fifties and sixties, you will not likely increase your spending much. That is the time of life when you must aggressively save for your retirement. Therefore, assume for the purposes of estimating your retirement spending that income growth will end at age 55, and that your income will remain constant for the rest of your career. The income you achieve at that time is an important number for your financial plan: we call it your Peak Net Income.

"Let's do some math and see how this works. Joe is age 23. He will be age 55 in 32 years, so we'll assume his gross income will grow at three percent per year for 32 years. We use the same formula for calculating his future gross income as we used to calculate future earnings for the College Fund. For Joe, whose current gross income is \$48,000, the formula is 1.03^{32} x \$48,000. The answer is approximately \$124,000. That is the best guess for Joe's gross income, in today's dollars, at age 55. To estimate his net income, we multiply that amount by 68%, which is the percent of gross income that typically falls to net income for a family with Joe's income level.[14] His Peak Net Income will be approximately \$84,000."

---

[14] Remember, we compute net income as gross income less federal and state income taxes, social security taxes, and health insurance premiums. Because of graduated tax rates, as income increases, the percentage of gross income which falls to net income decreases slightly. A chart showing the recommended percentage to use to convert gross income to net income is included in Appendix 2.

LET'S DO THE MATH

Age 55	55
Current Age	23
Years to Age 55	32
Annual merit income growth	1.03
1.03^{32}	= 2.58
Current Gross Income	$48,000
Expected Gross Income at Age 55	$123,604
(2.58 x 48,000)	
Net Income Rate	x 68%
(from Appendix 2)	
Expected Peak Net Income	$84,051

"I follow you on this calculation," said Mitchell. It seems the same as the one for college saving. For college, the EFC formula translated income directly to required cost. I know you said that retirement spending is linked to income. But is there a specific formula, like there was for college?"

"There is, and it is a much simpler formula than the formula that set your college EFC," answered the instructor.

He turned a page on the flip chart and wrote:

> ## STEP #15: ESTIMATE YOUR ANNUAL
> ## RETIREMENT SPENDING AT 65% OF
> ## YOUR PEAK NET INCOME

"How did you come up with that percentage?" asked Mark.

"Simple," answered the instructor. "During most of your life you will spend 90% of your net income. Of that 90%, the largest component is housing, which normally accounts for 35% of your net income. Most of that 35% - normally about 25% - goes toward paying your mortgage. Now, this is critical: when you retire, you must have paid off your mortgage. You cannot afford to make mortgage payments once you've retired."

Quite a few hands shot into the air. Sally spoke first, just beating a few others: "How can we pay off our home if we have to wait so long before buying one?" she asked emphatically.

The instructor expected that response. He remembered well the housing discussion, and how Sally and many others had been dismayed to learn that they would need to defer buying a home. He hadn't then touched on the impact of delaying your home purchase on retirement saving, but the subject couldn't wait much longer.

"Not only must you have paid off your mortgage to retire," he told them, "you probably must pay it off many years before you retire. A major portion of the contributions to your Retirement Fund are typically made just prior to retirement, when you have paid off your home and can redirect money that had been dedicated on mortgage payments into your Retirement Fund."

Lots of hands went up again.

"I know this is important to you. I promise we will address the interplay between paying off your mortgage and saving for retirement. Please bear with me until we're ready for the subject of contributing to your Retirement Fund. We need to set the target for your Retirement Fund before we tackle contributions to it. And to set the target, we need to estimate what you must spend each year."

There were some grumblings, but no objections, so the instructor went on with his explanation.

"Let's circle back to Mitchell's question about how to calculate retirement spending based on your pre-retirement income. While you will own your home debt free, you will still need to pay real estate taxes, insurance, assessments, and maintenance costs on your home. These should only amount to roughly ten percent of your pre-retirement net income. That cuts your expenses down to 65% of your pre-retirement net income as long as you maintain the same spending levels in all the other categories."

"I don't know that you can assume that ten percent would be enough for everybody," disputed Mark. "There are so many factors that affect what you'll have to spend on your house. You can't control your real estate taxes or your assessments or even your maintenance costs. It's possible that those costs could be fifteen or even twenty percent of your net income when you retire. Wouldn't that throw off this whole calculation?"

Mark was not alone in sensing a high degree of imprecision in this process. The instructor understood that there would be widespread skepticism, and he tried to bring people along point by point. "Certainly, not everyone will be exactly ten percent. Remember, we didn't expect everyone to spend exactly 35% of their net income on housing throughout their lives. The percentages for each spending category are a guideline to help you manage your expenditures so that they total 90% of your net income during your working life.

"During retirement, the 90% target drops to a 65% target. The target for housing is 10% of Peak Net Income. People's actual housing expenditures may be as low as 5% or as high as 15% or more. They need to adjust their spending in the other categories so that their overall spending equals 65%."

Mark was not quite convinced yet. "It's easy to say that they need to adjust their spending, but what if they can't do it?"

"It actually shouldn't be a struggle for most people. Does anyone see why?"

People thought for a few moments. "I think I do," Eric said. "Someone who spends more than 10% of their income on those housing costs in retirement probably was spending more prior to retirement, too. They would have been compensating all along by spending less than the target amount in some other category. They won't be forced to cut back in retirement; they can just continue to spend in the way they have always spent."

"What if they weren't spending less in other categories? What if they just spent more than 90% of their net income each year?" asked one man.

"Then they probably can't retire anyway, right?" answered Eric.

The instructor paused for a moment to allow everyone to consider Eric's argument. From the looks on their faces, they were beginning to understand.

"I know that the idea of specifically forecasting your retirement expenditures seems farfetched. If you accept that you don't need a perfect prediction, the exercise appears much more reasonable. You use your predicted expenditures as the basis for setting a Retirement Fund Target. Setting that Target accomplishes two goals: it allows you to create a savings plan during your working years, and it helps you know when you are financially able to retire. Let's continue with Joe as an example and you'll see better how this works.

LET'S DO THE MATH

Age 55	55
Current Age	23
Years to Age 55	32
Annual merit income growth	1.03
$1.03^{32} =$	2.58
Current Gross Income	$48,000
Expected Gross Income at Age 55	$123,604
(2.58 x 48,000)	
Net Income Rate	x 68%
(from Appendix 2)	
Expected Peak Net Income	$84,051
Target Expenditure Rate	x 65%
Target Retirement Expenditures	$54,633

The instructor continued his explanation: "We now have a reasonable estimate of what Joe will need to spend each year during his retirement, roughly $55,000. Remember, this is all in today's dollars. And of course it is subject to his having a fairly "normal" career path. If his income grows more or less than projected, he will need to adjust his retirement expenditures."

Something was bothering Sally: "I understand how you have put this together, but Joe is so young, there are bound to be major changes in his life you haven't captured. What if he gets married? Wouldn't that change the calculation entirely? He would have another person's income, and together they'll need more money to retire."

"That's a critical point," said the instructor. "This forecast is the best you can do now, with today's information. When you have a major change in your life: new job, a marriage, a divorce – anything that changes your income expectations, you need to recalculate. If Joe marries and his wife earns $100,000 per year, they need to add their incomes together to calculate a combined expected Peak Net Income. That recalculation will require a change in their plan for contributing to their Retirement Fund. For now, though, the best he can do is use his current status to forecast the future."

The instructor took a deep breath, pausing to allow the class to process everything discussed so far. When he felt they were ready, he continued: "You now know how to answer the first key question: how much money you will spend each year in retirement. We can move onto the second question: how long you will be retired? After answering that question, you will know how much money you'll need to support your retirement."

"That's not an easy question," said Mark. "The earlier you retire, the longer you will be retired. The longer you are retired, the more money you'll need. The more money you'll need, the longer you need to work, and the more difficult it is to retire early. It's a circular question."

"Mark, that's a very logical argument. The only way to deal with that challenge is to begin the process of creating a retirement plan using an assumed retirement age, and adjusting that retirement age later if necessary. I suggest using age 67 as your target retirement age, as that is currently the normal retirement age for Social Security."

Mark remained a little skeptical: "That seems a little cookie-cutter to me. Not everyone will want to retire at age 67 and spend 65% of their Peak Net Income. Some of us may prefer to retire earlier, or some of us may want to travel the world and will require more spending money. How do you account for these individual differences?"

The class nodded their heads in sympathy. They each had their own unique visions of their retirement. The instructor had expected that concern. "Don't worry, you will all be able to tailor your plan for your preferences. To create your Retirement Savings Plan, you need a starting point. As we develop your plans, we will discuss the feasibility of spending more or less, as well as choosing to retire earlier or later."

"You might be able to choose when to begin your retirement, but you can't choose when to end it," said Mitchell with a smile. To me, that is the biggest problem with this exercise. I don't have an issue with predicting my income, especially since, at my age, I don't expect it to increase much before I retire. And I have a good feel for how much I'll need to spend, too. But if you can tell me how long I'm going to live, then you've solved my problems. Otherwise, it's still a guessing game."

"Aren't there actuarial tables that can tell you how long you're going to live?" asked Andrea. "That's how life insurance companies know what to charge you."

"Sure," replied Mitchell passionately, "but that only tells you the life expectancy of the population as a whole. It doesn't say anything definite about me and my wife. We can't afford to spend all our money on the assumption that neither of us outlives our life expectancy."

"No, you sure can't," agreed the instructor. "But Andrea has a point, too. Life expectancy can help you understand how much you'll need during retirement. Start with the basic facts. The current average life expectancy for men is 75 years old and for women is 80 years old."

"Does that mean that a man who retires at age 67 should expect to be retired for eight years?" asked one man.

"It doesn't," said the instructor. "Life expectancy increases as you age. By making it to age 67, a person's life expectancy increases. For a man 67 years old, his life expectancy is 82 years. A woman's is 85 years."

"A man who retires at age 67 should expect to be retired for fifteen years. That's a big difference," said the man.

"I don't think fifteen years is enough," argued Mitchell. Fifteen years is the average, right? There's a 50-50 chance a man lives more than fifteen years. He needs to plan for that. You can't just get to age 82 and say, okay, I'm out of money, I'd better die now."

"Sure, but you need to be reasonable. There is probably some miniscule chance that you'll live to age 110. You can't try to save enough for that, or you'll never be able to retire," disputed Mark.

"Here are a few more statistics," offered the instructor. "Maybe we can use them to reach some consensus. A 67-year old man, has a 20% chance of living to age 90 and an 8% chance to live to age 95. A 67-year old woman has a 28% chance of living to age 90 and a 12% chance of living to age 95."

"Those are pretty low odds," said Mark.

"They are low," conceded Mitchell, "but I have a fear of outliving my money. What if my wife or I are one of the ones who do make it to 95?"

It was hard to contest Mitchell's point. "I see what you are saying," said Eric, "but don't people usually spend less when they reach their 90s? I have a grandmother who is 92, and she used to be much more active than she is now. She doesn't spend as much as she did ten years ago because she just can't do as much."

"Eric is right," said Mark. "You are assuming that you'd spend the same amount forever. But you could reduce your expenditures as you get older, when living into your nineties becomes a more real possibility.

"I guess so," said Mitchell reluctantly. "I'd still be worried, though."

"There's no precise answer to this question," said the instructor, looking to bring the discussion to a conclusion. "You need to save enough so that Mitchell's fear, that he outlives his money, is highly unlikely. Mark is right, too, though: you can't set your Target so high that it is impossible to achieve or you will never retire. As you age, as Mark says, you may need to adjust down your annual spending.

"The ability to adjust your expenditures during your retirement is a significant advantage that you have in planning for retirement compared to planning for college. That flexibility helps you accept the 'risk' of living beyond expectations. Given these competing considerations, let me propose a happy medium. For someone retiring at age 67, a 25-year retirement expectation offers considerable cushion. That is enough to carry you to age 92 without changing your spending, more than long enough for most people, but not so long that your Retirement Fund Target will be unattainable.

"I don't know. Twenty-five years of retirement seems like a lot," said Eric. "I can't imagine how I could save enough to retire for 25 years. It seems out of the question."

"I think you might be pleasantly surprised," said the instructor. "Let's take a break. When we return, we'll take the next step forward, and set a target for your Retirement Fund."

CHAPTER SIXTEEN

Setting a Retirement Fund Target

During the break, people were unable to turn their attention away from the class discussion. The idea of funding their living expenses for 25 years after retiring seemed impossibly daunting. A number of the participants had continued the discussion on their own during the break, and each person's recitations of his own fears intensified the angst in the rest. When they returned, they wanted answers.

Eric spoke for the group when he said to the instructor, "I don't see how Sally and I can retire. It will be over twenty years before we can start saving for retirement. After paying off debt, buying our cars outright, saving for a larger house, and putting our children through college, we'll be in our fifties before we can put a dime into our Retirement Fund. Then we need to accumulate enough savings to spend 65% of our income for 25 years? It's mathematically impossible!"

The instructor, who had planned to cover the topic of funding retirement expenses next, found Eric's question a perfect lead-in. He said to Eric, "If your Retirement Fund were to be the sole source of funding for your retirement expenses, I think you might be right. Fortunately, for most of you Social Security will provide a substantial portion of the money you will spend in retirement. Social

Security reduces the savings burden and makes retirement possible for people who otherwise could not retire."

"Social Security?" exclaimed Mark. "Come on, we all know Social Security is running out of money. We can't depend on Social Security being there when we retire."

"Mark's right," supported Joe. "It seems to me we should ignore Social Security, because, chances are, at least for people my age, we're not going to see any of that money."

The instructor had expected skepticism when he mentioned Social Security. "I'd say we're ready to discuss Question #3: -- how much income you will receive from Social Security. It's clear there is a general uncertainty about the U.S. Government meeting its commitments under Social Security. We hear frequently from the media and from politicians that Social Security is going bankrupt, or that it's broken and needs to be fixed. It is fashionable for financial management gurus to tell you not to count on Social Security.

"But most of you can't ignore Social Security. You will need it to retire. Instead, you need to ignore the propaganda, take a realistic look at Social Security, and do your best to forecast what you can expect to receive when you reach retirement age.

"Wait a second," said Jack. "Forecasting Social Security benefits is different than forecasting income growth or investment growth. You can't just take historical data and project it forward. Congress will have to change the laws governing Social Security, and there is no way to 'project forward' what they will do. It's a political decision. It's fundamentally unpredictable."

The instructor shook his head. "While you make some relevant points, your conclusion is wrong. Like the other forecasts, our forecast for Social Security is subject to error. If and when we learn that our prediction turned out wrong, we'll need to adjust our savings plans. But we *can* make reasonable predictions regarding Social Security payments. In fact, we can make better predictions for Social Security than any other aspect of our retirement plans.

First, to understand how Social Security laws may change, we need to recognize the issues plaguing Social Security now." He turned to the class and asked: "What are the dynamics that are putting financial pressure on the Social Security system?"

A few hands went up. "The ratio of workers to retirees is shrinking," Joe offered. "The baby boomers are beginning to reach retirement age. That will boost the number of retirees who collect Social Security and reduce the number of people employed and paying Social Security taxes."

"People are living longer, too," added Bruce. "The longer they live, the longer they receive their Social Security benefits."

"Great," said the instructor. "Joe and Bruce have nicely summarized the problem facing Social Security. There are two basic ways to fix Social Security's finances: either raise the Social Security tax or cut Social Security benefits. To make Social Security solvent, the tax would need to increase by 1.7%. Currently, the combination of the employer tax and the employee tax is 12.4%. Raising that tax to 14.1% would solve the entire problem without any reduction in retiree benefits."[15]

The instructor's statement was greeted with silence.

"Really? Are you sure?" eventually Bruce asked with amazement. His surprise was mirrored in the faces of most of the rest of the students, most of whom had imagined that a much larger tax increase would be necessary.

The instructor pressed on: "If Congress chooses not to raise the tax rate, it could instead reduce the benefit rate. An 11.5% cut in the benefits of all workers and retirees would also solve the entire problem without any increase in taxes."

"Eleven and a half percent doesn't sound so small," said Mitchell.

---

[15] These projections were made in an April 2008 paper by the AARP Public Policy Institute. A link to the paper is available at www.dougwarshauer.com.

"Maybe not," countered Eric, who was beginning to see in Social Security a ray of hope, "but I think the point is that 11.5% is a lot less than 100%, right? There's no way Social Security will be eliminated if it only takes a 11.5% reduction in benefits to make it solvent."

"Right," said the instructor. "Social Security is not going away. Most likely, Congress will eventually address the solvency issue by some combination of increasing the tax and decreasing the benefit. If they split the difference, people's benefits would fall five or six percent below their current level."

"That's an average for everybody, isn't it?" Joe noted. "Chances are everyone won't be treated the same. Young people will have a larger reduction than people at or near retirement age. Since I won't reach retirement age for about 45 years, I could get nailed with much more than a five or six percent reduction in benefits."

"Very true," commented the instructor.

He walked over to the flip chart. "When Congress last restructured Social Security in 1983, it raised the normal retirement age gradually from 65 to 67. People of different ages were, in fact, affected very differently. People over 45 years old were not impacted at all, while people under age 23 – who for the most part had not yet begun to work – received a 13% reduction in benefits. Based on that experience and our understanding of the magnitude of the changes necessary to make Social Security solvent, we can make a good guess at how the upcoming changes will eventually affect you. I will write a chart for how much I suggest that you decrease your estimated Social Security benefit because of likely future changes in the statute. This is my best guess. If and when the statute is actually changed, you'll obviously want to update your calculations."

TABLE 16-1

Age	Reduction
50 and over	3%
40-49	6%
30-39	9%
20-29	12%

"Aren't your percentages arbitrary?" asked Joe.

"They are, in that, as Jack has shown us, they are not extrapolations of historical data. But they are reasonable in light of the economic facts and political realities. Most important, they are unlikely to be wrong enough to matter much. Suppose people in their 40s receive a 10% reduction instead of a 6% reduction. For a family who expected to receive $40,000 in Social Security, they would receive $1,600 less. That variation is negligible compared to the likely error in forecasting changes in your income or your investment rate of return. Of all the variables that affect your retirement savings plan, Social Security is the most predictable."

"Are you saying that I should expect a 12% reduction in my Social Security benefit, but if it turns out to be a little more or less than that, it's not a big deal?" Joe paraphrased.

"Exactly," said the instructor.

One man looked confused. "I don't understand what you mean by 'percent reduction'," he said.

"I mean the percent of the amount you would receive under current Social Security law," replied the instructor.

"Honestly, I have no idea what I would receive under current Social Security law," said the man.

The instructor sighed. "Almost no one does. I will teach you how to estimate what you will receive according to today's law. Pretend you have reached age 67, the current normal retirement age.[16] Your Social Security benefit depends upon the gross income you earned in your 35 highest paid years prior to your retirement. Before calculating what you earned each year, the Social Security Administration will adjust for inflation each year's actual earnings by an Index factor. The top 35 adjusted earnings are then averaged. The result is your Average Indexed Earnings.

"Once you know your Average Indexed Earnings, determining your annual Social Security payment is easy. You will receive 90% of the first $8,928 of Average Indexed Earnings, 32% of the next $44,868, and 15% of all additional Average Indexed Earnings."

"Looking at that formula, it's clear that you don't benefit much from earnings over $54,000," said Eric.

"That's right. Let's look at a few examples so you see how this works. If your Average Indexed Earnings are $10,000, you will receive a benefit of $8,378. If your Average Indexed Earnings are $30,000, you will receive a benefit of $14,778. At $50,000 Average Indexed Earnings, you will receive a benefit of $21,178. Much above that average, your benefit only increases fifteen cents for every dollar, and it maxes out at a benefit of $30,344 if your average is above the maximum of $106,800. If your Average Indexed Earnings are $75,000, your benefit would be $25,574."

"I think I understand the calculations," said the man, "but I still couldn't figure out what I receive. I have no idea what my earnings were for the last 35 years. Even if I did, I wouldn't know the Index factors to use."

---

[16] The normal retirement age is lower for people born before 1960. If people born before 1960 retire at age 67, as we assume in this book, they will receive somewhat larger Social Security benefits. A chart showing the percentage increase in their benefits is included in Appendix 3.

"Not to worry," answered the instructor. "The Social Security Administration periodically sends you a statement showing your earnings each year. If you haven't saved your most recent statement, you may request a new one from them. The statements don't show the Index factors, but I will pass out a chart showing them for each year.[17] Any other questions?"

No one answered, so he continued. "Now that you have a feel for how this works, let's take a look at some real examples. Joe, let's continue with you for a while. Because Joe is just starting his career, we have to forecast his earnings forward. We know he is starting with gross income of $48,000. We need to estimate the amounts he will earn each year over his entire career, and we need to estimate them in today's dollars, because, remember, all of his retirement savings calculations will be done in today's dollars.

"To make these estimates, we can continue to assume that Joe receives a 3% merit increase each year until age 55, just like we did when we forecast his retirement spending requirements. Everyone with me?"

Everyone looked both with him and very focused, so he continued: "Here the math gets a little laborious, but not difficult. We take Joe's gross income for this year, $48,000, and multiply it by 1.03. That equals $49,440, his gross income for next year. Multiply $49,440 by 1.03 to calculate his gross income in two years. Multiply that number by 1.03 to calculate your gross income in three years. Continue doing this 32 times. The final twelve years are easy, because we'll assume no income growth between age 55, when he reaches his Peak Net Income, and age 67, his retirement age.

"We have now forecast Joe's gross income every year for the rest of his career. To calculate his Average Indexed Earnings, because Social Security only counts earnings up to $106,800, for any year Joe earned more than that, we use $106,800 as his earnings. We're

---

[17] The chart of Index factors in included in Appendix 4.

almost done. We then take the average of the final 35 years, which will be his highest paid years. To take the average, add the gross income from each of those years and divide that sum by 35. The result is Joe's Average Indexed Earnings."[18] According to this calculation, Joe's Average Indexed Earnings are approximately $95,000. He will receive an annual Social Security Benefit of approximately $29,000.

"Really," said Joe with some surprise. "That's not bad."

"But you need to reduce that amount for expected changes to Social Security laws, right?" asked Bruce.

"Right," agreed the instructor. "Joe is between 20 and 29, so we should reduce his benefit by 12%. Reducing $29,000 by 12% leaves approximately $25,000. That is our best estimate of what Joe will receive from Social Security when he reaches retirement age."

---

[18] This calculation can be done on a pocket calculator, and while it may take 30 minutes, it is a worthwhile use of time. Also, a spreadsheet specifically tailored for this purpose is available at www.dougwarshauer.com.

LET'S DO THE MATH

Age	Gross Income	Social Security Income	Age	Gross Income	Social Security Income
23	48,000	48,000	46	**94,732**	**94,732**
24	49,440	49,440	47	**97,574**	**97,574**
25	50,923	50,923	48	**100,501**	**100,501**
26	52,451	52,451	49	**103,516**	**103,516**
27	54,024	54,024	50	**106,622**	**106,622**
28	55,645	55,645	51	**109,821**	**106,800**
29	57,315	57,315	52	**113,115**	**106,800**
30	59,034	59,034	53	**116,509**	**106,800**
31	60,805	60,805	54	**120,004**	**106,800**
32	62,629	62,629	55	**123,604**	**106,800**
33	**64,508**	**64,508**	56	**123,604**	**106,800**
34	**66,443**	**66,443**	57	**123,604**	**106,800**
35	**68,437**	**68,437**	58	**123,604**	**106,800**
36	**70,490**	**70,490**	59	**123,604**	**106,800**
37	**72,604**	**72,604**	60	**123,604**	**106,800**
38	**74,782**	**74,782**	61	**123,604**	**106,800**
39	**77,026**	**77,026**	62	**123,604**	**106,800**
40	**79,337**	**79,337**	63	**123,604**	**106,800**
41	**81,717**	**81,717**	64	**123,604**	**106,800**
42	**84,168**	**84,168**	65	**123,604**	**106,800**
43	**86,693**	**86,693**	66	**123,604**	**106,800**
44	**89,294**	**89,294**	67	**123,604**	**106,800**
45	91,973	91,973			

Average Indexed Earnings	$95,029
(Social Security Income ages 33 – 67, years in bold)	
Annual Social Security Benefit	$28,578
Deduction for Expected Changes to Social Security Laws	12%
Net Estimated Social Security Benefit	**$25,149**

"What if your forecast is wrong? Joe himself acknowledged that he doesn't know where his career will end up," said Sally.

"For Social Security, it hardly matters," answered the instructor. "No matter how much better Joe does, he won't get much more Social Security. Even if he does worse than this projection, he won't get much less. Suppose his earnings grow only 2% per year instead of 3%. That may not sound like a big difference, but it results in an ending gross income of about $90,000 instead of $124,000. That change would reduce Joe's spending expectations in retirement by about $15,000 per year, but it will only reduce his Social Security benefit by about $2,000 per year! I'll say it again: forecasting your Social Security benefit is less subject to error than any other part of your retirement plan."

"Joe is not married, so this question isn't relevant to him, but how does it work with a spouse? Do both people get benefits?" asked one man.

"They do. Let's look at Mitchell this time. You'll be able to see how the spouse plays into the calculation. Mitchell's gross family income, as we saw last week when we looked at saving for college, is $120,000. That amount is the sum of Mitchell's earnings and his wife's. I asked Mitchell to bring his Social Security Statement with him today so that I could use him as our example, and he graciously agreed.

"Now that you know how the calculation is done, I will let you in on a secret. Mitchell's statement does the work for him. On page two, under a section called 'Your Estimated Benefits', it tells him the monthly payment he will receive if he continues working until he reaches his full retirement age. According to his statement, he will receive $2,000 a month, or $24,000 per year."

"Wouldn't that change if my income changes going forward? The Social Security Administration can't know what I'll earn the next ten years," said Mitchell.

"True," agreed the instructor. "For you, however, it doesn't matter much. They assume you'll earn in the future about what you've earned the last two years, which is what we forecast for you, too. Also, as we saw with Joe, a small change in your earnings will hardly affect your benefit at all. You can rely on the number in the statement as a good predictor of your benefit."

"Mitchell can use his statement," said Eric, "because he is toward the end of his career. For me, being only 30 years old, I would need to use the more laborious method that you showed us for Joe, right?"

"That's right," said the instructor. "Anyone under 45 probably ought to use the longer method."

"What about Mitchell's wife?" asked one woman. "You said that Mitchell's calculation is different than Joe's because he is married."

"Right. As long as his wife has worked at least a minimal amount," replied the instructor, "she'll have a Social Security Statement, too. Mitchell can add her benefit to his to calculate his family's total benefit."

"What if Mitchell's wife didn't work outside the home. Would she still get a benefit?"

"She would. The spouse with the lower benefit level will always receive a benefit of at least 50% of the higher earning spouse's. If Mitchell's wife worked very little over her lifetime, she would receive half Mitchell's benefit level."

For a moment, everyone was silent. So much ground had been covered, the participants tried to mentally assimilate it all. Their thoughts were interrupted by Bruce, who hit on the last major issue related to Social Security. "What about taxes?" he asked. "Aren't Social Security payments subject to tax?"

"Some are," answered the instructor. "Currently, about 40% of people who receive Social Security benefits pay a tax on them. Everyone else pays no tax."

"Why are some people taxed on them but not others?" Bruce followed up.

"That's the law. Here's how it works: If your family income is below $32,000, you don't pay any tax on your Social Security benefits. In calculating your income, Social Security benefits count only fifty cents on the dollar. For example, if you have $20,000 of employment income and $16,000 of Social Security benefits, the Social Security benefits only count as $8,000. Adding the $8,000 to the $20,000 equals $28,000, which is under the $32,000 minimum necessary to make Social Security benefits taxable. You would pay no tax on your benefits. People who don't have much other income, and that is the case for most retired couples, don't pay any tax on their benefits."

"If your gross income is between $32,000 and $44,000, you will pay some tax on your Social Security benefit, but it will be quite small. You will probably pay less than ten percent of your benefit in tax. Even at income levels above $44,000, only 85% of your benefit will be taxed, so at a tax rate of 25%, you would lose about 20% of your Social Security benefit to taxes. If your benefit would have been $50,000, you'll keep $40,000 of it."

"That is pretty complicated. We don't know exactly what our income will be when we are retired, do we?" asked Bruce.

"Maybe not, but as long as you retire by age 70, most of you won't pay much tax. The Social Security Administration allows you to wait until you are 70 years old to start receiving your benefit, and it increases your future benefit because of that delay. If you don't want to retire at your full retirement age, or if you can't afford to retire at that age, don't take your benefit. You do not want to begin taking your Social Security benefit until you retire. If you continue working once you begin receiving benefits, the regular income you receive will put you over the limits, and you'll pay tax on your Social Security benefit.

"Once you are retired, you should have very little taxable income. Your investments will produce some income, but not too much. If they are in tax-deferred accounts like a 401k or IRA they'll produce even less. In fact, for many of you the bulk of your taxable income each year will come from the withdrawal of your money from tax-deferred accounts. Here is a rule of thumb: if you expect your Peak Net Income to be less than $100,000, you can ignore the possibility of taxes on your Social Security benefits. You will probably pay none, and if you do pay some they will be negligible."

At this point, the instructor stood up and returned to the flip chart. He continued speaking: "If you expect your Peak net Income to be between $100,000 and $150,000, use this graduated chart as a guideline to reduce your expected Social Security benefit due to the effect of taxation.

TABLE 16-2

Impact of Taxes on Social Security Benefits:

Expected Peak Net Income	Reduction in after tax SS benefit
Less than $100,000	0%
$100,000 - $115,000	5%
$115,000 - $130,000	10%
$130,000 - $150,000	15%
Greater than $150,000	20%

"My head is spinning," said Eric. "Everything you tell us make sense when you are saying it, but I'm having trouble seeing where this is all going."

He wasn't alone. The complexity of dealing with Social Security, its laws, prospects, and taxes, was trying the patience of the entire group. The instructor recognized the need to wrap the discussion together. "I understand this is a struggle. Let's refocus on the big picture. Before the break we calculated how much money you will need to spend each year when you retire. A portion of your spending will be supported by Social Security. You need to estimate how much Social Security will cover in order to know how much savings you'll need.

"Estimating your Social Security benefit depends on four factors: one, your Average Indexed Earnings; two, the formula that translates those earnings into your benefit; three, the tax rate you will pay on your benefit; and four, the possibility of changes in the Social Security laws that would reduce your benefit. We have now discussed all four factors. Let's go back to our examples and put it all together.

"According to Mitchell's Social Security Statements, his annual benefit will be $21,000 and his wife's will be $16,000. Together, their family benefit will be $37,000. Because Mitchell is currently 55, and his family's net income is under $100,000, he should not have to pay any material taxes on his Social Security benefits. Because Mitchell was born between 1943 and 1954, his full Social Security retirement age is 66 instead of 67. By electing to begin receiving benefits at age 67, he will receive an 8% increase in his benefit amount. However, because Mitchell and his wife are in their fifties, the expected impact of future changes in Social Security laws dictates that he reduce their expected benefit by 3%. Thus, their final after-tax family Social Security benefit will be 5% more than $37,000, or approximately $39,000.

"Let's put that together with their retirement spending forecast. Their current net income is $81,600. They are currently 55, so they can assume they are already at their Peak Net Income. Their spending budget in retirement will be 65% of $81,600 which is approximately $53,000. So, they will need to spend $53,000 and Social Security will support $39,000 of that spending. The rest, $14,000 needs to be supported by other sources."

LET'S DO THE MATH

Mitchell's Expected Annual SS Benefit	$21,000
Wife's Expected Annual SS Benefit	$16,000
Total Expected Annual SS Benefit	$37,000
Deduction for Taxes on SS Benefits	0%
Increase for birth date between 1943-1954	+8%
Deduction for Expected Changes to Social Security Laws	-3%
Net Increase to Annual SS Benefit	5%
Net Expected Annual SS Benefit	$38,850
Peak Net Income	$81,600
Expenditure Rate	65%
Annual Expenditures in Retirement	$53,040
Annual Expenditures in Retirement	$53,040
Less Net Expected Annual SS Benefit	$38,850
Annual Unsupported Retirement Expenses	**$14,190**

"So that's what they need their Retirement Fund to cover?" asked one man.

"Yes, that's exactly right. You now know how to perform Step #16A."

He turned to the flip chart and wrote:

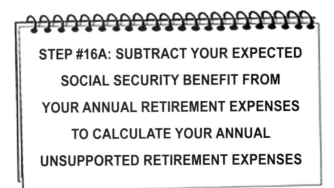

STEP #16A: SUBTRACT YOUR EXPECTED
SOCIAL SECURITY BENEFIT FROM
YOUR ANNUAL RETIREMENT EXPENSES
TO CALCULATE YOUR ANNUAL
UNSUPPORTED RETIREMENT EXPENSES

"Now I understand why you told us not to ignore Social Security," said Eric. "Mitchell will have almost three-quarters of his retirement expenses supported by Social Security. Without Social Security, he'd have to save four times as much money as he will actually need."

Mitchell had a smile as wide as the Pacific Ocean. "I was thrilled by last week's class, but this is even better. When I came to this seminar a few weeks ago, I wasn't sure I could pay for either college or retirement. Now it's possible I can do both."

The instructor allowed the class to vicariously enjoy Mitchell's excitement for a moment before continuing the discussion. He flipped the chart back to the page with Joe's numbers. "Let's go back to Joe and calculate his Annual Unsupported Retirement Expenses. Before the break we saw that he had Target Retirement Expenditures of approximately $55,000. We have projected his Peak Net Income below $100,000, so he too can disregard taxes on his Social Security benefits. But at age 23, he needs to reduce his benefit by 12% for likely changes to the Social Security laws. Thus, while we calculated his Social Security benefit at approximately $29,000, he should expect to receive roughly $25,000. The difference between his spending, $55,000, and his Social Security benefit, $25,000 is $30,000. That is the amount he will need to support with his Retirement Fund."

LET'S DO THE MATH

Average Social Security Income ages 33 – 67	$95,029
Annual Social Security Benefit	$28,578
Deduction for Expected Changes to Social Security Laws	12%
Net Estimated Social Security Benefit	$25,149
Peak Net Income	$84,051
Expenditure Rate	65%
Annual Expenditures in Retirement	$54,633
Annual Expenditures in Retirement	$54,633
Less Net Expected Annual Social Security Benefit	$25,149
Annual Unsupported Retirement Expenses	**$29,484**

"Wait a second. Joe's income when he is Mitchell's age is supposed to be about the same as Mitchell's. Why will he need his savings to support twice as much spending as Mitchell will?" asked Sally.

"Great question," said the instructor. "Can anyone explain why?"

"I think so," said Mark. Joe is younger, so we are reducing his projected benefit by 12% instead of 3%."

"That's part of it," agreed the instructor, "what else?"

"Joe isn't married. For the same family income, you get a much larger benefit if you have two wage earners instead of one," Andrea pointed out.

"Precisely," said the instructor. "If Joe were to get married, even if his wife never worked and generated any income, they would, as a family, get a 50% larger Social Security benefit than Joe will receive on his own. It's a good reminder as to why you need to recalculate your retirement plan upon any major life event."

The instructor paused for a moment to prepare for a change in the discussion. They had spent considerable time on Social Security, and he wanted to move on. "You are ready to calculate your Retirement Fund Target," he said.

He turned to the flip chart and wrote:

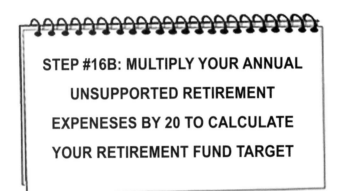

STEP #16B: MULTIPLY YOUR ANNUAL
UNSUPPORTED RETIREMENT
EXPENESES BY 20 TO CALCULATE
YOUR RETIREMENT FUND TARGET

"Why 20 and not 25? I thought you need to plan for a 25 year retirement," Jack said.

"You do, but your Retirement Fund Target only needs to be about 20 times the annual spending that the Retirement Fund must support. Can anyone figure out why?"

Everyone thought for a moment. "It must be that you expect the money invested in your retirement fund to grow while you are retired," offered Joe.

"That's right," said the instructor.

"Hold on," Mitchell called out. "You're not going to tell us we should be investing in equities after we're retired, are you?"

While Mitchell appeared astonished by that thought – he still had not fully overcome his aversion to investing in equities – most of the class seemed far less surprised. Mark spoke for them: "It makes sense when you think about the Time Horizon. If we are planning on a 25 year retirement, we must have a 25 year Time Horizon, right?"

"True," said Sally, "but you also have a one year Time Horizon, since you will spending at least some of the money in your Retirement Fund each year." She turned to the instructor and asked, "You're not suggesting we should have all our Retirement Fund invested in equities, are you?"

The instructor shook his head emphatically. "Of course not. Around the time you retire, you should reduce the allocation of equities in your Retirement Fund to approximately 50%. This allocation provides ample ability to support your living expenses without selling any equity investments for quite a while."

He turned to the flip chart and began writing. "Every three years after retiring, you should reduce the percentage of equities by 10%."

TABLE 16-3

Age	Percentage of Equities in Retirement Fund
67	50%
70	40%
73	30%
76	20%
79	10%
82	0%

"When we were discussing the College Fund, you told us not to sell the equities if they were down? Does that rule apply here, too?" asked Andrea.

"It certainly does," the instructor answered, "for the same reason, too. You only have a 25 year Time Horizon if you are willing to use it. If your equities have not kept pace with the rate of inflation, defer any planned sale until they catch up."

"I'm still not comfortable with that plan," Mitchell complained. What if your equities keep falling and you never sell them. Eventually you'll have spent all the money you had in fixed income investments and you'll have to start selling your equities in order to live, won't you?"

"As I always tell you when we discuss investing, there are no guarantees," said the instructor. "But you should be reassured that under normal circumstances investing your Retirement Fund in this manner will support your expenses for 28 years, not 25, so you will have built in a three-year cushion. In the event that your Retirement Fund begins to run out, either because of poor investment returns or any other reason, you will have a significant backstop: the equity in your home. If you have been following the lifetime financial plan we have discussed, in most circumstances when you die your heirs will inherit your home free of debt. If however, you have a financial emergency late in life, when it is otherwise impossible for you to go back to work, having a debt-free home is the ultimate security blanket."

"I understand what you are saying, but I'm just having trouble accepting it. What if I wanted to invest all my Retirement Fund in fixed income investments?" Mitchell asked.

"You could do that, but you'd need a larger Retirement Fund," the instructor answered. "Your Annual Unsupported Retirement Expenses are $14,000 per year, so you have a Retirement Fund Target of $280,000 ($14,000 x 20). If you planned on using only fixed income investments, you would want to multiply $14,000 by 25 instead of 20. You'd need $350,000 in your Retirement Fund to retire."

"Wow," said Mitchell, "that's a big difference."

"Let's take a break again. When we come back, I will show you how to calculate the percentage of your net income you'll need to contribute to your Retirement Fund each year in order to achieve your Retirement Fund Target."

CHAPTER SEVENTEEN

Creating a Retirement Savings Plan

Many of the students didn't leave their seats during the break. Instead, they punched their own numbers into their calculators and notebook computers, using their new knowledge to calculate their own Retirement Fund Targets. Determining how much they would need to retire would have seemed impossible only an hour ago. Now, as they pecked at their keyboards, they felt on the verge of achieving the ultimate goal -- a thorough, consistent, and achievable lifetime financial plan.

The instructor needed three attempts to capture everyone's attention, so busy were they manipulating their own numbers. Finally, with everyone's eyes on him, he said, "A little review. We began today with three key questions that make calculating your Retirement Fund Target difficult. One, how much money will you spend each year you are retired, two, how long will you be retired, and three, how much income will you receive from Social Security?

"Now that you know how to answer those questions, you are each capable of setting your Retirement Fund Target. Setting the Target is half the battle. The other half, creating a plan that will enable you to achieve that Target, we can discuss now."

Jack listened to the instructor at the same time he continued to fiddle with his numbers. He looked worried. In fact, were he not dubious of the accuracy of his calculations, he might have looked despondent. Almost without looking up, he said, "I hope I'm doing something wrong. The Retirement Fund Target I calculated seems impossible to achieve, especially with all our savings going to our Auto and College Funds for the next twenty years.

"I doubt it's impossible," the instructor encouraged. "It may seem that way now, looking at a big number without the road map to achieving it."

He turned to the flip chart and wrote:

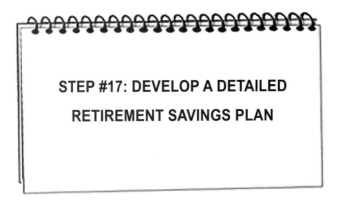

**STEP #17: DEVELOP A DETAILED
RETIREMENT SAVINGS PLAN**

He turned to the class: "To create a detailed Retirement Savings Plan, begin by dividing your Retirement Fund Target by your Peak Net Income. For example, if your Retirement Fund Target is $500,000, and your Peak Net Income is $100,000, your Target is five times your Peak Net Income. Go ahead and calculate your own number."

The class made their own calculations. After a few moments, the instructor asked: "What numbers did you come up with?"

"Four."

"Seven."

"Two-and-a-half."

"Nine."

"What about yours, Jack?" asked the instructor.

He and Isabel had been whispering to each other about their numbers. "Ours is a little more than ten," he said.

"That's what I'd have guessed," said the instructor knowingly. "This number you just calculated is a key component of your retirement savings plan. The higher your number, the more resources you must devote to your Retirement Fund?"

"So I was right," said Jack glumly. "Our number is higher than everyone else's. Why is that?"

"Does anyone have a guess?" the instructor asked the class.

"Their income is high," answered Mark. "Social Security covers more of the retirement spending of people with lower incomes. For Jack and Isabel and the rest of us with higher incomes, our Retirement Funds have to do most of the work."

"That's exactly right," said the instructor. "There is a direct relationship between your Peak Net Income and the Number of Times Peak Net Income you must save. Fortunately for those of you with higher Peak Net Incomes, including Jack and Isabel, you should have the ability to save the necessary amount. Ready to see how?" Everyone assented enthusiastically, so the instructor continued: "Most of you will have two main sources for contributions to your Retirement Fund. The first source is the most obvious: you can put some or all of your Annual Savings into a 401(k), IRA, or some other vehicle designed for retirement savings."

"Right, but according to what we've learned so far, most of us can't start doing that for a while," moaned Eric. "We have Auto Funds, Home Funds, and College Funds, too."

"Very true. Don't worry; we won't ignore that when we develop your retirement savings plans. Eventually you will be able to put some of your Annual Savings into your Retirement Fund. In fact, once you have finished putting your kids through college, you'll probably be able to put all your Annual Savings into your Retirement Fund."

"Maybe, said Eric, "but our Retirement Fund Target is seven times our Peak Net Income. I don't see how saving ten% of our net income would ever get us close, even if we were to start now. Since we can't save for retirement for close to twenty years, we don't have a chance."

"If Annual Savings were your only source for Retirement Savings, you would have a problem. Fortunately, it isn't the only source. In fact, for many people it isn't even the most important source. Remember our discussion earlier today about the importance of paying off your mortgage well before you reach retirement age? The other source of contributions to your Retirement Fund is the money that you had been spending on your mortgage payment, once you have paid off your home."

The hands shot up. A number of people started to talk but Sally's passionate voice was heard above the crowd. "How can we have paid off our home in time to save for retirement? You don't have us buying another home for at least seven more years. We're only thirty now, but by then we'll be thirty-seven. If we take out a 30-year mortgage, we'll be sixty-seven when it's paid off! That's not when you want us to start saving for retirement, is it?"

"I'll be older than that," added Bruce. "My mortgage won't be paid off until I'm in my seventies."

Although much of the class seemed to support Sally and Bruce, another faction offered an alternative. Andrea spoke for them. "You don't need a 30-year mortgage. I have a 15-year mortgage on my house. I chose it to force myself to save. Plus, the interest rate was a little lower than a 30-year mortgage would have been."

"I don't know," Sally responded, "we are going to want as much house as we can afford. A 30-year mortgage makes our money go farther."

"Actually, it doesn't," countered the instructor. "A 30-year mortgage encourages you to buy *more* house than you can afford. It's similar to taking out debt. You sacrifice your future to spend more in the present. Eric is right that you cannot retire solely on the basis of your Annual Savings. You need to pay off your house long before you plan to retire.

"Let me show you what happens if you take out a 15-year mortgage instead of a 30-year mortgage. You said you'll be 37 when you buy your house, right?"

"Right," Sally assented.

"With a 15-year mortgage, you will be only 52 when you own your home debt free. You will have 15 years to save for retirement using the money you previously spent on your mortgage. As we did when calculating your retirement spending, we'll assume that paying off your mortgage frees up 25% of your net income. By contributing 25% of your net income to your Retirement Fund for 15 years, you will accumulate about five times your Peak Net Income. Since you need to reach seven times your Peak Net Income to achieve your Retirement Fund Target, this source of savings accomplishes 5/7 of your goal."

"So their Annual Savings would only have to accumulate to two times their Peak Net Income?" asked Joe, with surprise.

"That's right. Most people think of their Annual Savings as their primary source of Retirement Fund contributions. They shouldn't. Your Annual Savings has a number of other 'jobs' to do. By the time you can devote it strictly to your Retirement Fund, you will be too old to save enough to retire on schedule. But paying off your mortgage and diverting that money toward your Retirement Fund for ten or fifteen years before you retire will make retirement possible for all of you."

"Can you explain how you calculated that Eric and Sally could accumulate five times their Peak Net Income that way?" asked Jack.

"Of course. Let's do a little math. During the fifteen years prior to their retirement, Eric and Sally will contribute ¼ (25%) of their net income to their Retirement Fund. As they will be ages 52-66 during this time, their net income will be either their Peak Net

Income or very close to it each of those years. Therefore, without any interest they will have contributed nearly 15/4, or 3 ¾, of their Peak Net Income to their Retirement Fund.

"In addition, they will earn interest on those funds for fifteen years. Their Time Horizon is long enough for them to invest 70% of those funds in equities. Given the assumptions regarding the rate or return on equity and debt that we discussed a few weeks ago, their investment return should be more than 1 ¼ times their Peak Net Income. All told, they will have a bit over 5 times their Peak Net Income after fifteen years."

He went to the flip chart and turned a page, revealing a table which he proceeded to explain: "This table shows how Eric and Sally's, or anyone's, savings grows over fifteen years. While shown for a family with a Peak Net Income of $100,000, it would produce identical results regardless of the Peak Net Income. As you can see, each year the family contributes 25% of its net income to its Retirement Fund. The balance in the fund grows each year by the new contribution plus investment growth. The final column, "Number of Times Peak Net Income," tells us what we want to know. A family who contributes to its Retirement Fund in this way for 15 years, as Eric and Sally will, finishes with more than five times Peak Net Income in the fund.

TABLE 17-1

Year	Net Income	Investment Growth	Contribution	Ending Balance	Number of Times Peak Net Income
1	91,514	-	22,879	22,879	0.2
2	94,260	1,071	23,565	47,514	0.5
3	97,087	2,224	24,272	74,010	0.7
4	100,000	3,464	25,000	102,473	1.0
5	100,000	4,796	25,000	132,269	1.3
6	100,000	6,190	25,000	163,459	1.6
7	100,000	7,650	25,000	196,109	2.0
8	100,000	9,178	25,000	230,287	2.3
9	100,000	10,777	25,000	266,064	2.7
10	100,000	12,452	25,000	303,516	3.0
11	100,000	14,205	25,000	342,721	3.4
12	100,000	16,039	25,000	383,760	3.8
13	100,000	17,960	25,000	426,720	4.3
14	100,000	19,971	25,000	471,691	4.7
15	100,000	22,075	25,000	518,766	5.2

"That's great for Eric and Sally," said Joe, "because they will buy their house when they are 37 years old. What happens if you are older? You encouraged us to wait to buy our first house until we could stay in it until we are confident we'll stay there for ten years, right?"

"That's right," agreed the instructor.

"Suppose I don't buy my first house until I am 35, then I stay there for ten years. I'll be 45 when I buy the second house. You see where I'm going? Even with a 15-year mortgage, I'll be 60 when I pay it off. At that point, I won't have 15 years before retirement, I'll only have seven."

"You're right," agreed the instructor. "Not everyone will be in exactly the same position." He pointed at the table on the flip chart. "Look at Year #7. It tells you how many times Peak Net Income you will have saved at the end of the seventh year."

"Well," said the Joe, "it looks like I would only be able to save 2 times my Net Peak Income instead of the 5 times that Eric and Sally will save. "Does that mean I should reconsider whether it is a good idea to wait so long before buying a house in the first place?"

"Not necessarily," responded the instructor. "Eric and Sally need to rely very heavily on this source of retirement saving because they bought their house early, probably too early. They can't use their Annual Savings to contribute to their Retirement Fund for a long time. You may be better able to use your Annual Savings. Let's take a closer look at that method of Retirement Fund saving.

"Joe, suppose you can to begin contributing to your Retirement Fund when you are 30 years old. Does that sound reasonable?"

"I don't know," Joe answered. "I need to spend the next two years paying off debt, and the next two years after that on my Auto Fund. By then I'll be 27, and I still need to contribute to my Home Fund, right?"

"That's right," agreed the instructor. "Let's suppose you contribute 10% of your Net Income to your Home Fund for three years, until you are 30, then you begin to split your Annual Savings between your Home Fund and your Retirement Fund, and even perhaps your College Fund if you have a child by then."

"Can you really split your savings in all three ways and still accomplish anything?" asked Isabel.

"If you are only 30 years old, you probably can," answered the instructor. "A 30-year old only needs to contribute 1.5% of his net income to his Retirement Fund for the rest of his career in order to finish with 1 times his Peak Net Income."

"He needs to contribute it every year, though, not just when he is 30, right?" clarified one woman.

"Right. If Joe were to begin contributing to a 401k plan at age 30, and continue contributing until he retires at age 67, and each year he contributed 1.5% of his net income, when he retired he would have in his fund 1 times his Peak Net Income."

"Does that include the employer match?" asked Joe.

"It does. If your employer matches 100% of your contribution, you would only need to contribute 0.75% of your net income, and the employer match would make your total contribution to your Retirement Fund 1.5% of your net income."

"What if Joe needs to save more than 1 times his peak net income? How does he know how much he needs to contribute then?" asked one man.

"It would be proportionate, wouldn't it?" answered Bruce. "If he needs to save twice his Peak Net Income, he needs to contribute twice as much. He'd need to contribute 3.0% per year to his Retirement Fund, right?"

"Exactly," said the instructor.

He turned a page on the flip chart, revealing Table 17-2.

Table 17-2
Impact of Annual Contributions to
Retirement Funds Beginning at Age 30

Percent of Net Income Contributed	# of Times Peak Net Income
1.5%	1
3.0%	2
4.5%	3
6.0%	4
7.5%	5
9.0%	6
10.5%	7

"Using Tables 17-1 and 17-2, we're ready to look at Joe's retirement plan in detail now." He turned the page on the flip chart and began writing Joe's numbers for all to see. "You will see how it all fits together. Before the break we determined Joe's Retirement Fund Target was approximately $600,000. His Peak Net Income is expected to be approximately $84,000. Dividing $600,000 by $84,000 gives us about seven. Joe needs to accumulate about seven times his Peak Net Income. Let's figure out how he can do that."

"We just said that I would be able to save two times my Peak Net Income after paying off the mortgage," Joe interrupted. "That's still what we are assuming, right?"

"Yes, let's stick with that," agreed the instructor.

"So I need my Annual Savings to add up to five times my Peak Net Income, don't I?" he proposed.

"That's exactly right. Keep going," encouraged the instructor.

"We said I'd start contributing to my Retirement Fund when I'm age 30. According to this chart, if I need to accumulate five times my Peak Net Income, I need to save 7.5% of my net income each year."

"Including employer matches, right?" Sally looked for clarification.

"Right," said the instructor. "His personal contribution could be reduced by the amount of his employer's matching contribution.

"So, if I understand this right," said Joe, "here is my retirement plan: I contribute 7.5% of my net income to a 401k plan beginning at age 30 until I retire. Also, I make sure that I have paid off my home by the time I'm 60 years old, so that I can contribute an additional 25% of my net income for seven years before retirement. That's all I need to do?"

"Based on your current expectations for your future income, yes," agreed the instructor.

LET'S DO THE MATH

Retirement Age	67
Age Mortgage will be paid off	60
Years of Retirement Saving	7
Number of Times Peak Net Income	**2**
(from Table 17-1)	
Age Beginning 401k Contributions	30
Percent of Net Income Contributed	7.5%
Number of Times Peak Net Income	**5**
(from Table 17-2)	
Total Number of Times Peak Net Income	**7**

"Wait a second," said Jack. "That sounds easy now because Joe doesn't have any children. But once he has children, saving 7.5% of his net income each year may not be possible. Like the rest of us, he might have to put most of his savings into his College Fund."

"But other things would change, too, if he had children," countered Sally. "He'd probably be married, and his wife might have an income."

"He and his wife would also receive more money from Social Security, wouldn't they?" Mitchell pointed out. "Didn't you tell us that even a non-working spouse gets at least half the other spouse's Social Security benefit? That would reduce the size of his Retirement Fund Target, so maybe he wouldn't need to save as much per year?"

The instructor felt very gratified by the discussion. Everyone had come a long way from the first meeting. "I can see you are learning. Joe's plan looks very achievable now, but he will need to modify his plan as major changes occur in his life. Those changes may present different challenges, but they will not make retirement unreachable, as long as he modifies his retirement plan appropriately. Let's look at some examples of people who do have to plan around College Fund contributions, and also who don't have the luxury of beginning to make Retirement Contributions at age 30."

"Can we go back to us?" asked Sally plaintively. We started talking about what we needed to do but we didn't finish."

"Sure," said the instructor. "Like Joe, you need to save seven times your Peak Net Income. By paying off your house by age 52, you can redirect your mortgage to contribute to your Retirement Fund, and that will get you to five times your Peak Net Income. You need to use your Annual Savings for the rest."

"But we can't start when we're 30 years old," Eric pointed out. "Since we're starting later, we will need to contribute a higher percentage of our income, won't we?"

"You do," agreed the instructor. He turned the page on the flip chart again. "Here is another table that you will find useful. It shows how the percent of your net income which you must save annually to accumulate one times your Peak Net Income increases according to the age you begin saving."

Table 17-3	
Beginning Age	**Percent of Net Income Required to Save 1X Peak Net Income**
30	1.5%
35	1.9%
40	2.5%
45	3.3%
50	4.7%
55	7.5%
60	14.6%

"Wow," said Mitchell, "it really starts shooting up there as you get older."

"That's right," agreed the instructor. "It's clearly better to start younger, but the difference between 30 and 35 is small. The longer you wait, the more challenging it becomes to get much mileage out of your Annual Savings."

Eric was looking at the chart and feverishly calculating his own numbers. When he finished, he looked encouraged, if still a bit unsure. "We aren't going to make any contributions until we are 50," he said. "At that point, though, we'll be done paying for college and can put all our Annual Savings into our Retirement Fund. Since we need to reach two times our Peak Net Income, we should need to save 9.4% of our net income per year, right? Two times 4.7%?"

"Exactly right," said the instructor.

"That's cutting it a little close," said one man. "Don't you want a little more cushion than that?"

"I agree," said another. "There are a lot of assumptions involved in these calculations. If they turn out to be wrong, Eric and Sally may not have enough to retire, after all."

"There certainly are a lot of assumptions," agreed the instructor. "It is possible that you could follow your Retirement Plan and not reach your Retirement Fund Target. In a few minutes, we'll talk about what you do if that happens. First, I want you to see a few more examples so you fully understand how to create a Retirement Plan. Let's look at Mitchell next."

Mitchell looked up when he heard his name. He had been working through his own numbers on his calculator. The instructor flipped back to the page with Mitchell's numbers. His Retirement Fund Target was $280,000, and his Peak Net Income was about $82,000. Mitchell said, "I need to save about 3.5 times my Peak Net Income, right?"

"Right," said the instructor. "Let's see how you can do it. First, when will your house be paid off?"

"Not for another eight years," Mitchell answered. "That only leaves me four years to use the money from my mortgage payments for Retirement Savings. According to Table 17-1, I only reach one times my Peak Net Income for that."

"Yes. What about using your Annual Savings?"

"Most of it will be tied up in college savings for the next six years. I will be over age 60 when my Annual Savings can go into my Retirement Fund. According to your chart, even contributing all 10% into the Retirement Fund won't get us to 1 times my Peak Net Income."

"No, you're right. You need 14.5% for one times; contributing 10%, you will only get about 2/3 of that. But, if you have a company match you may get to one times. Do you?"

"Yes, they match up to 3% of my gross income."

"That will get you about 4.5% of net income. Add that to the 10% of net income you will contribute and you should be right around 14.5%. Together, those contributions should grow to approximately 1 times Peak Net Income."

"Good. That gets me to two times," said Mitchell. "I still need to be at 3.5 times."

"What about savings you have already put away? Do you have anything in your or your wife's 401k now?"

Mitchell brightened. "I sure do. We have been putting in some money over the years."

"And you didn't include that money last week in the savings for your kids' college education?" the instructor confirmed.

"No, this money is in our 401k plans. Between the two of us, we have about $70,000. That gets us closer."

"Not just closer," said the instructor happily. "That's all you need. Don't forget, you have twelve years to invest that money before your retirement." He turned the page on the flip chart and revealed yet another table. "Here is one last table. This tells you how much you can expect your current savings to grow between the present and your retirement, depending on your current age."[19]

Table 17-4

Future Value of Current Savings

Age	Multiple of Current Value As of Your Retirement Date
62 or over	1.0
61	1.1
60	1.2
59	1.3
58	1.4
57	1.5
56	1.6
55	1.7
54	1.8
53	1.9
52	2.0
51	2.1
50	2.2
49	2.4
48	2.5
47	2.7
46	2.9
45	3.0
44	3.2
43	3.4

Continued

---

[19] The calculations in the chart use the same rate of return for both equity and fixed income investments that we have used throughout the book. Asset allocation of 70% equity/30% fixed income after age 57, 85% equity/15% fixed income from 52-57, and 100% equity prior to age 52.

42	3.6
41	3.8
40	4.0
39	4.2
38	4.4
37	4.6
36	4.8
35	5.0
34	5.3
33	5.5
32	5.8
31	6.0
30	6.3

"Mitchell, who is 55, can expect his current savings to grow by a factor of about 1.7. His $70,000 will have turned into approximately $120,000 when he is ready to retire."

Mitchell quickly realized that $120,000 is about 1.5 times his Peak Net Income of $82,000. "Wow. I think I'm okay then. I'll get 1 times from using my mortgage money, 1 times from my Annual Savings after my kids are out of college, and 1.5 times from my existing savings. That adds up to 3.5 times my Peak Net Income!"

LET'S DO THE MATH

Retirement Age	67
Age Mortgage will be paid off	63
Years of Retirement Saving	4
Number of Times Peak Net Income	**1**
(from Table 17-1)	

Age Beginning 401k Contributions	60
% of Net Income Contributed	14.5%
Number of Times Peak Net Income	**1**
(from Table 17-3)	

Age	55
Multiple on Current Balance	1.7
Existing Balance in Retirement Fund	$70,000
Expected Balance at Retirement	$119,000
Peak Net Income	$82,000
Number of Times Peak Net Income	**1.5**
(from Table 17-4)	

Total Number of Times Peak Net Income 3.5

Bruce didn't look satisfied. "I hate to throw cold water on Mitchell's celebration, but it still seems like he's cutting it close. What if his $70,000 savings doesn't grow to $120,000? We all know that there is no guarantee that in 12 years it will have grown at all."

"True enough," agreed the instructor. "He has a very good chance, but not a certainty, of having enough money to retire at 67. If at that age he hasn't accumulated $280,000 in his Retirement Fund, he will have options. I know you are curious about those options, but we need to look at more examples of building a Retirement Savings Plan first. Andrea, you're next. Tell us all your numbers."

Andrea perked up: "Sure. I forecast my Peak Net Income at about $65,000. My Retirement Fund Target is about $350,000. So I need to save about 5 ½ times my Peak Net Income."

"Perfect. Where is it going to come from?"

"As I said earlier, I have a 15-year mortgage on my house. I just closed on my house a few months ago, so I'll have it paid off in fifteen years when I'm 55. That will leave me 12 years before I'm age 67. According to Table 17-1, I'll be able to save close to four times my Peak Net Income once the mortgage is paid off."

"Very good," said the instructor. "Go on."

"I need to save about 7% of my net income for my College Fund. I also need to pay down debt and start an Auto Fund, so there is no way I'll be able to save anything for retirement until my daughter finishes college in 11 years. I'll be just over 50 years old then. At that age, saving 4.7% per year would get me 1 times my Peak Net Income, so if I need 1 ½ times my Peak Net Income, I should save 1 ½ times 4.7%, right?"

"Exactly," said the instructor, impressed with her understanding. "Go on."

"Well, 1 ½ times 4.7% equals about 7%. That's the amount of my Net Income I will need to save each year, beginning at age 50."

LET'S DO THE MATH

Retirement Age	67
Age Mortgage will be paid off	55
Years of Retirement Saving	12
Number of Times Peak Net Income	**4**
(from Table 17-1)	
Age Beginning 401k Contributions	50
% of Net Income Contributed	7%
Number of Times Peak Net Income	**1.5**
(from Table 17-3: 7% ÷ 4.7%)	
Total Number of Times Peak Net Income	**5.5**

"Beautiful," said the instructor. "You did that perfectly. And everyone note that Andrea will only need Annual Savings of 7% from the time she's 50 years old to reach her target. She actually can build up an even larger Retirement Fund than she needs."

He paused for a moment. "Okay, one more before we break. Jack and Isabel, let's look at your numbers."

Jack and Isabel had been whispering to each other. Jack said, "I see that everyone else's retirement plans seem to work, but our numbers just don't add up. At least, they don't add up to us having enough money to retire. It's like I said earlier – our Retirement Fund Target seems impossible to achieve."

"Tell us your numbers and we'll see what you can do," said the instructor.

"All right," Jack agreed. "We forecast our Peak Net Income at about $230,000. Our Retirement Fund Target is about $2,300,000. So we need to save 10 times our Peak Net Income. That is far more than anyone else has needed to save."

"You can be sure any of us would be happy to have $2,300,000" said one man pointedly.

"Right," said the instructor. "Keep in mind that the objective of your retirement plan is to enable you to maintain the lifestyle you achieved prior to retirement for the rest of your lives. People with higher incomes will have higher expectations for their lifestyle in retirement. Realizing those expectations may take a little more work."

"So what do we do?" Isabel asked.

"Start with your home. When will you have that paid off?"

"We don't know," said Isabel. "We're still in our first home. We have been planning to move to a new home in a few years."

"How old do you think you would be when you buy your new home?"

"I guess around 40," answered Isabel.

Jack made a few calculations: "If we take out a 15 year mortgage, we'd be 55 when we pay that off. That would leave us 12 years until we're 67, the same as Andrea. We could save about 4 times Peak Net Income, right?"

"Right," said the instructor. "What about Annual Savings?"

"Here's where we run into trouble," said Jack. "We have to save 10% of our net income for the next 20 years to pay for college. We've got nothing left to save for retirement until the kids finish college. By then we'll be 55."

"You're right," said the instructor. "If you wait until you're 55, you will have a real problem. To save the 6 times Peak Net Income you still need, you'd have to save 45% of your net income each year!"

LET'S DO THE MATH

Retirement Age	67
Age Mortgage will be paid off	55
Years of Retirement Saving	12
Number of Times Peak Net Income	**4**
(from Table 17-1)	
Age Beginning 401k Contributions	55
% of Net Income Contributed	*45%*
Number of Times Peak Net Income	**6**
(from Table 17-3: 7.5% x 6 = 45%)	
Total Number of Times Peak Net Income	**10**

"So we can't retire, right? There's now way to get close to our number," Isabel moaned.

"It may look that way, but it's not nearly as bad as it seems. This is a perfect time for a break. When we come back, we will look at how Jack and Isabel can craft a retirement plan that will work for them. We'll also discuss the various options I've been promising Bruce. These are the options that any of you will have available if the retirement plan that you put together fails to achieve its objective."

CHAPTER EIGHTEEN

Making Your Retirement Plan Work

An observer wandering through the halls outside the classroom during this final break would have noticed a stark dichotomy between two classes of people. The first, larger class appeared to float on air, so buoyant were their spirits. These fortunate people knew their lifetime financial goals were within their grasp. Their calculations demonstrated that they could afford to send their children to college and save for retirement. The confidence they felt relieved the burden of stress that had weighed them down for as long as they could remember.

In marked contrast, a handful of people appeared slumped, discouraged, and absorbed by concern for their future. The considerable knowledge they had acquired in the seminar left them more downbeat than they had been five weeks earlier. Their destiny, instead of a great unknown, appeared now as an ocean of unachievable goals. Their calculations seemed to prove that they would not be able to save enough money to pay for college, or to retire, or both. With only minutes remaining in the seminar, they doubted they would find a resolution to their predicament.

As the participants re-entered the room at the end of the break, the instructor addressed his comments to the second group: "I know that a few of you are thinking 'why did I come here, if only to learn that my goals are out of reach?' This final part of the class is for you. For those of you lucky enough to know that you can comfortably meet all your financial goals by simply saving ten percent of your net income and investing it wisely, you will derive even greater comfort from the remainder of today's class, as you'll learn about back-up plans you could employ in the event of unexpected financial duress. For those of you who need to do more than save ten percent per year, you will see that you still have quite a few options. If you feel discouraged right now I promise you will feel better before you leave this room."

"Why is it that most of the people here only need to save ten percent, but a few of us need to save more?" asked one man, who from his body language clearly fell into the discouraged group.

"Most people, if they begin saving ten percent of their income young enough, and if they invest it as we've discussed, can accomplish all their goals by sticking with that simple program. Unfortunately, some people who begin saving too late in life, or who have overspent and run up too much debt, or who have invested very poorly, may find that they do not have enough time left before their normal retirement age to pay off their debt and accumulate the necessary savings. People with higher incomes, who cannot rely on College Financial Aid or Social Security to provide much assistance, are more likely to face this predicament.

"If saving ten percent a year will not accomplish all your goals, you still have lots of options. To see some of these options, let's revisit Jack and Isabel's situation. Remember, if Jack and Isabel follow our basic program, saving ten percent per year, they won't be able to begin saving for their retirement until they reach age 55. Starting so late, they could not accumulate enough savings to reach their Retirement Fund Target. Does anyone have any suggestions for what they need to do to escape this quandary?"

"I do. You said their Retirement Fund Target was $2,300,000. That's more than double what my wife and I need. They could just lower their target," James said pointedly.

Bruce didn't agree with James. "I don't think telling them to 'just lower their target' is much of a solution. The targets allow people to maintain their lifestyle. When I retire, I want to take vacations, play golf, and do everything I don't have time for while I'm working. Why retire if you can't afford to do what you want? I'd rather keep working until I can afford it."

"That sounds great, except you might be working forever," James responded.

Andrea had a different approach: "What if Jack and Isabel saved more than ten percent each year?" asked Andrea. "With a Peak Net Income of $230,000, if they save ten percent they have over $200,000 to spend. They could save 20% and still have a lot more to spend than most of us."

"Your right, Andrea," said Mitchell. "If Jack and Isabel want to build their Retirement Fund to $2,300,000, they have to save more than ten percent a year. Maybe they need to save 20% a year, like you suggested. Maybe even more. If they save so aggressively, they will need to live a more restrained lifestyle when they are working, right? But James has a point, too. They may not need such a high target. Saving enough to reach a target of $2,300,000 would allow them to live better after retirement than they did before. That wouldn't make sense, would it?"

Jack and Isabel sensed that a solution to their problem may be approaching. Isabel said, "I agree, that wouldn't make sense. Shouldn't we figure out how much we need to save each year so that our spending while we work matches our spending in retirement?"

"Exactly," said the instructor. "For most people, ten percent is that magic number. People like you in the highest income brackets, however, will often need to save more."

"How do we figure out the right number?" Isabel followed up.

"It's not hard," said the instructor. "You adjust your Annual Savings rate in conjunction with the percent of your Peak Net Income you will spend in retirement. Normally, we assume 90% spending while you work (10% Annual Saving) and 65% spending in retirement. If those percentages don't allow you to achieve your Retirement Fund Target, recalculate your Retirement Plan, assuming Annual Savings of 15% each year and retirement spending of only 60%. Do you see how this remains balanced, keeping spending during your working life aligned with spending in retirement?"

"I don't get it – how does it remained balanced?" asked one woman.

The instructor explained it carefully: "Remember, we set your retirement spending expectations at 65% of your Peak Net Income because that allows you to maintain roughly the same spending budget you had prior to retirement. Now, if you reduce your pre-retirement spending budget by 5% of your net income, because you must save more of your money, you can similarly reduce your post-retirement spending budget by 5% of your Peak Net Income. That means you base your Retirement Fund Target on a spending expectation of 60% of your Peak Net Income instead of 65%."

"Ok, I understand that," said Isabel. So we have to recalculate the whole plan, right?"

"Let's do it," said the instructor. "Your Peak Net Income was about $230,000. Sixty percent of that is $138,000. Subtract your estimated Social Security benefit of…"

"$32,000" answered Jack.

"Which means your Retirement Fund must support about $106,000 of annual spending. Multiply that by 20 and your Retirement Fund Target is $2,120,000, $180,000 less than before. Divide $2,120,000 by your $230,000 Peak Net Income, which equals a little more than 9 times your Peak Net Income. Before your target was 10 times your Peak Net Income. Your savings goal is more reachable."

"Not that much more," said Isabel disappointedly. "I was hoping it would have dropped more than that."

"That's only half the story," said the instructor. "Your saving ability is now much greater. As before, assume you can save four times your Peak Net Income after you pay off your home. You now need your Annual Savings to accumulate to five times your Peak Net Income. Can you do it?"

Jack thought for a minute. "Since we will save 15% each year, we could begin putting 5% into our 401k right now. My employer would match half that, so we'd get credit for 7.5% of our net income, right?"

"Right," said the instructor encouragingly.

Jack flipped through his notes. "According to Table 17-3, you accumulate 1x Peak Net Income for every 1.9% of your net income you contribute if you begin at age 35. Since 7.5% is about four times 1.9%, we should reach 4x Peak Net Income. We'd be 1x Peak Net Income short."

Isabel brightened visibly. "But when we're 55 and done paying for College, we could start putting more into the Retirement Fund, too. How do we count that?"

"Add it separately," answered the instructor. "Contributing 10% of your net income beginning at age 55 will accumulate to a little more than 1 times Peak Net Income. That puts you over the top."

Jack, too, looked dramatically more upbeat: "So what you're saying is we can retire as long as we save 15% of our net income each year?"

"I didn't say it – you figured it out. Correctly."

LET'S DO THE MATH

Retirement Age	67
Age Mortgage will be paid off	55
Years of Retirement Saving	12
Number of Times Peak Net Income	**4**
(from Table 17-1)	
Age Beginning 401k Contributions #1	35
% of Net Income Contributed	7.5%
Number of Times Peak Net Income	**4**
(from Table 17-3: 7.5% ÷ 1.9% = 4)	
Age Beginning 401k Contributions #2	55
% of Net Income Contributed	10%
Number of Times Peak Net Income	**1**
(from Table 17-3)	
Total Number of Times Peak Net Income	**9**

"That's great for Jack and Isabel. But what would they do if saving 15% wasn't enough for them to retire?" asked Mark.

"Anyone have an answer to Mark's question?" asked the instructor.

"I suppose they could recalculate their plan using Annual Savings of 20% a year," said Sally.

"Sure," said the instructor. "You can keep recalculating your plan until you get one that works. You don't have to use 5% increments, either. If your plan almost works at 10%, you could try saving 12% annually and spending 63% of your Peak Net Income. That small change may be enough to make your plan work."

He paused for a moment. "Congratulations, we have reached the final step."

He turned to the flip chart and wrote"

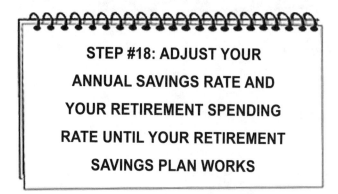

STEP #18: ADJUST YOUR
ANNUAL SAVINGS RATE AND
YOUR RETIREMENT SPENDING
RATE UNTIL YOUR RETIREMENT
SAVINGS PLAN WORKS

"I suppose if you do this, at some point, everyone will be able to find a savings level that works for them on paper," said Mark. "That doesn't necessarily mean they can do it. "If Jack and Isabel needed to save 25% of their net income, they might find it impossible to cut their spending enough."

"True," agreed the instructor. "Jack and Isabel are young enough to have over 30 years of saving left. If they were older, the required Annual Savings rate might be impossibly high."

"That's my point. What would they do then?" Mark followed up.

"To help you see what they could do, let's return to Mitchell. When we discussed Mitchell's numbers, Bruce pointed out, rightly, that Mitchell's plan didn't seem to leave a lot of room for error."

The instructor turned the flip chart back to the page with Mitchell's retirement plan. "Mitchell needs to save 3.5 times his Peak Net Income. He can save one times his Peak Net Income after paying off his house at age 60, and another 1 times from contributions to his 401(k) that will begin around age 60. He also has existing money in his 401(k) that he expects to amount to 1.5 times his Peak Net Income. The sum of all those sources equals his goal of 3.5 times Peak Net Income. Of course, if any of them fall short, he will not reach his Retirement Fund Target."

LET'S DO THE MATH

Retirement Age	67
Age Mortgage will be paid off	63
Years of Retirement Saving	4
Number of Times Peak Net Income	1
(from Table 17-1)	
Age Beginning 401k Contributions	60
% of Net Income Contributed	14.5%
Number of Times Peak Net Income	1
(from Table 17-3)	
Age	55
Multiple on Current Balance	1.7
Existing Balance in Retirement Fund	$70,000
Expected Balance at Retirement	$119,000
Peak Net Income	$82,000
Number of Times Peak Net Income	1.5
(from Table 17-4)	
Total Number of Times Peak Net Income	3.5

"That's right," said Bruce. "I remember thinking that a number of things could go wrong. You said not to worry, that he had some options if they did go wrong."

"I did. We're ready now to look at those options. Let's pretend that Mitchell did not currently have any money in his 401(k)."

"So this is what I would do if I had saved nothing for retirement yet?" Mitchell asked.

"Right. Mitchell is 55 years old. Imagine he has saved nothing for retirement, and he cannot begin saving for five more years. He needs to save 3.5 times his Peak Net Income, and he will only be able to save two times it. What can he do?"

"He could save more," Eric commented. "Like Jack and Isabel raised their savings rate from 10% to 15%, Mitchell could do the same. That might solve his problem."

"True," agreed the instructor, "but let's also imagine that Mitchell looks at his expenses and determines he cannot possibly save more than ten percent per year. He still has options. Any thoughts on what they are?"

"Sure," said Mark, a bit sarcastically, "he could keep working."

"Yes!" shouted the instructor earnestly. "If you can't retire at your normal retirement age, you can keep working. We need to figure out how long Mitchell would need to keep working past his normal retirement age. Any ideas?"

No one answered immediately.

"Come on people, the answer is right in front of your faces. Mitchell's Retirement Fund is short of its Target by 1.5 times his Peak Net Income. How many years extra does he need to work?"

"One and a half years?" Joe ventured uncertainly.

"Yes! Each year he works he earns his Peak Net Income. If he's 1.5 times short, he needs to work 1.5 years. That is the beauty of using this method of retirement planning. You can easily tell how many extra years of work are required for any shortfall in your Retirement Fund."

LET'S DO THE MATH

Retirement Age	67
Age Mortgage will be paid off	63
Years of Retirement Saving	4
Number of Times Peak Net Income	**1**
(from Table 17-1)	
Age Beginning 401k Contributions	60
% of Net Income Contributed	14.5%
Number of Times Peak Net Income	**1**
(from Table 17-2)	
Actual Retirement	68.5
Planned Retirement Age	67.0
Extra Years of Work	1.5
Number of Times Peak Net Income	**1.5**
Total Number of Times Peak Net Income	**3.5**

The class took a moment to think about that concept. It certainly made sense. Still, it seemed almost too easy.

"I'm finding this a little hard to believe," said Bruce. "You are telling us that if Mitchell never saves a dime for his retirement until he is 60 years old, he could still retire only 1.5 years later than normal without ever saving more than ten percent of his net income."

"Yes," agreed the instructor, "as long as he pays off his house by the time he's age 60 and puts the money he had been spending on his mortgage into his Retirement Fund."

"I'm surprised, too," said Andrea. "I assumed if you waited that long to begin saving, you could never retire."

"You're not alone," agreed the instructor. "Most people underestimate the impact of working longer. If you understand how powerfully working a little longer can make up for shortfalls in your

Retirement Fund, you will worry less about the assumptions built into your plan. If, for instance, your equity investments do not earn the rate of return expected of them, you can probably make up the shortfall by working a few extra months."

If any uneasiness remained among the participants whose retirement plans already worked, this discussion dissolved it. Few, if any, of them had recognized the impact that a very modest deferral of retirement would have. Of course, for some people there was a downside to the importance of your retirement date. Mark asked: "Does that mean the opposite is true, too: early retirement is almost impossible?"

"It's not impossible," answered the instructor, "but it is awfully challenging. "Unless you work in a job with a generous defined benefit pension plan, you would need to save substantially more than ten percent per year throughout your career if you want to retire much before your normal retirement age."

"There's one thing I'm worried about," said Mitchell. "You are assuming you can keep working at your job as long as you want. What happens if you can't? What if your job has a mandatory retirement age, or if you physically can't continue to perform your job anymore?"

"Or what if you just get laid off?" added Sally.

"In other words, what if you have to retire, even if that isn't what you want to do?" clarified the instructor. "That can happen. You still would have a few options. First, you may be able to work part-time during your retirement. It's easy to determine how long you'd need to do that. Suppose you take a part-time job from which you earn 1/3 of your Peak Net Income. Working that job for three years during retirement would equal one year of delayed retirement. Make sense?"

"Sure, but what if you can't find part-time work? What then?" Sally pressed.

The instructor surveyed the room. "Who has an answer for Sally. What can you do if you have reached your retirement age, you have not reached your Retirement Fund Target, and you find yourself unemployed?"

"If it were me, I would cut back my spending," Mark proposed.

"Right, that seems obvious," agreed one man.

"Could you cut back enough?" asked Andrea. "Isn't the whole point of this retirement planning process that we not have to cut way back when we retire?" she asked pointedly.

"It is," replied Eric, "but we're talking about a worst case scenario. You'd have to be at retirement age, have failed to save enough, and be unable to find any reasonable job."

Eric's statement, though logically true, failed to satisfy people. They craved security, and the fear that the worst case scenario might apply to them prevented them from feeling fully confident in their plans.

"Couldn't you move to a less expensive house?" proposed Mark. "Lots of people downsize their houses when they retire." He turned to the instructor: "A few weeks ago when we discussed housing, you said we should think of owning three houses: a starter home, a primary home, and a retirement home. The retirement home would usually cost less than the primary home, right?"

"Right, Mark," said the instructor. "That is another reason it is critical to pay off your mortgage as soon as you can. For most people, their home is their ultimate safety net. If they need to, they can trade their primary home for a retirement home and typically pocket one to two times their Peak Net Income from the difference in value. It is an excellent alternative to working longer for people who either don't want to or cannot defer their retirement. Because retired people generally need less space, they can often move to a smaller home."

"Moving to a smaller home also helps cut your expenses. I'm looking forward to spending a lot less in real estate taxes, for one," Mitchell added happily.

"Couldn't you build downsizing your home into your Retirement Plan in the first place?" asked one woman.

"You could," answered the instructor, "but I discourage it. Let's review how you create your Retirement Plan. First, you estimate your Peak Net Income, carve out 65% of that as your annual retirement spending, and subtract your expected Social Security benefit to determine your Annual Unsupported Retirement Expenses. You then multiply that amount by 20 to arrive at your Retirement Fund Target.

"Once you have your Target, you divide it by your Peak Net Income so that you can build a plan to accumulate the required amount. You achieve your goal by 1) contributing to your Retirement Fund the money that you had been spending on your home mortgage, once your mortgage is paid off; 2) contributing as much of your Annual Savings that is remaining after first paying off debt, contributing to your Auto and Home Funds, and contributing to your College Funds, and 3) adding the estimated future value of any money you have already set aside for retirement.

"For most people, these three sources will be adequate to enable them to retire at their normal retirement age. If they are not adequate, you can raise the percentage of Annual Savings from 10% to a higher amount and correspondingly reduce the percentage of your Peak Net Income you expect to spend in retirement. Again, for most people, a reasonable change in these percentages will enable them to build a Retirement Plan that works.

"If you have begun this process too late in life, or if your current spending requirements are too inflexible, you may find it impossible to create a Retirement Plan that allows you to retire at your normal retirement age. In that case, deferring your retirement will probably solve your problem. A one or two year deferral of retirement can make a major difference and enable a family who did not begin saving until their sixties to retire. If you do not want to or cannot defer your retirement, you could instead work part-time during retirement.

"Finally, if you do not want to or cannot work part-time during retirement, you could trade your primary home for a less expensive retirement home. While you could build this trade into your initial plan, doing so will discourage you from saving the amount that you truly ought to save. Worse, it will eliminate your safety net. Remember, there are no guarantees. If you have a Retirement Plan that does not depend upon using the equity in your home, you can rest quite comfortably knowing that you have a substantial safety net that will enable you to have a long, comfortable retirement under virtually any circumstances."

* * * *

The instructor took a deep breath. He looked at the clock; the class had gone twenty minutes overtime. The participants seemed in no hurry to leave. They had learned so much, so quickly. They would need time to digest it all.

As they filed out of the classroom, their attention was torn between reflecting on the content of the seminar and saying fleeting goodbyes to each other. The class had bonded tightly over the personal and private financial secrets they shared with each other. Abruptly, it was over. Though a few had exchanged phone numbers, they would not likely meet again. They came from different walks of life, and what they shared in the seminar they could not replicate in the outside world.

As the instructor watched them leave, he contemplated how well he'd come to know them. Eric and Sally, whose mistakes with their housing investment had set them back years, left arm in arm.

Although they would have to wait longer than they'd like before moving to a larger house, they knew that they could eventually buy their dream home, that they could afford to send their two children to college, and that they could ultimately enjoy a comfortable retirement.

Andrea, who had constantly impressed him with her insight and perceptiveness, also had a bright future. Despite the obvious challenges as a single parent, she would have an easier time achieving her financial goals than almost anyone else in the class. She amiably chatted with Isabel as they left. Isabel and Jack's poor stock investing had heightened the challenges that accompany high income. At their income level, College Financial Aid and Social Security offered little assistance; they needed their own savings to carry the load. Nevertheless, their spirits seemed much higher than they'd been less than 30 minutes earlier. They had a road map that would enable them to achieve their financial goals.

Mitchell left with the same smile he'd worn the entire class. Even when worried, he looked happy. Still, the instructor noticed a difference in the way he carried himself. The stress that had once been evident in the hunch of his shoulders and the lines on his forehead had, if not completely disappeared, visibly diminished. With his children's college around the corner and his retirement not far behind, he had a confidence about his financial future he could not have imagined a few weeks earlier.

Joe was last to leave. At only 23 years old, he had wasted little time backing himself into a financial corner. Clearly very bright, and certainly sophisticated about banking and finance, the instructor wondered how he could have been so reckless with his personal finances. At the same time, he knew Joe was no aberration. Around the country millions of college graduates receive training in accounting, finance, and business but virtually no guidance at all managing their own financial lives.

Contemplating Joe made him wonder about the entire class. They were nearly all smart, successful people. They were concerned about their financial situation and eager to learn. Why, then, had nearly all of them dug themselves into a financial hole of one sort or another? Why had they never acquired the tools to successfully manage their financial lives?

The instructor considered what distinguished his class from other personal financial advice. Such advice is widely available, but its effectiveness was always limited by its generality. While people could understand the concepts, and perhaps even internalize them, they could not act upon them.

By contrast, each of the students in this seminar left understanding how to create a lifetime financial plan specifically for themselves. They could balance their various objectives and set specific financial targets for each one. They knew the amount they'd need to save, and how to invest the money they set aside. When he considered that everyone who passed through that door a few moments ago had come in the same door five weeks ago with their own unique problems, he recognized that a remarkable transformation had occurred.

As the instructor thought again about Eric and Sally, Andrea, Jack and Isabel, Mitchell, and Joe, he allowed himself to smile. Then he walked out the door, too, his mind on the next seminar and the people who he'd meet the next time.

THE 18 STEPS

BIG STEP 1: Control Spending and Debt

Step 1: If you are spending more than you are earning, you must either start earning more or spending less.

Step 2: Begin saving 10% of your Net Income every year.

Step 3: If you have credit card or consumer debt, use your Savings to pay off debt before Investing in anything else.

BIG STEP 2: Save for Short-Term Goals

Step 4: Once you have paid off your credit card and consumer debt, begin saving to achieve your short-term goals.

Step 5: Contribute your Annual Savings to your Auto Fund until you can buy your next car for cash.

Step 6: Do not buy a home unless you expect to live in it close to ten years.

BIG STEP 3: Invest Wisely

Step 7: Understand that Risk is the possibility of not being able to buy what you are Saving for when you want or need to buy it.

Step 8: Invest your Short-term Funds in fixed income securities.

Step 9: Select fixed-income securities to minimize credit risk and interest rate risk.

Step 10: When Investing in equities, buy index funds.

BIG STEP 4: Save for College

Step 11: Estimate your Expected Family Contribution for College

Step 12: Calculate your College Fund Target, and recalculate it every few years, or sooner if your income changes significantly.

Step 13: Follow the Recommended College Fund Asset Allocation, except do not sell your equity investments when they have a negative inflation-adjusted return.

Step 14: Use the College Savings Rate Table to set your annual college savings rate.

BIG STEP 5: Save for Retirement

Step 15: Estimate your annual retirement spending at 65% of your Peak Net Income.

Step 16A: Subtract your annual Social Security benefit from your annual retirement expenses to calculate your Annual Unsupported Retirement Expenses.

Step 16B: Multiply your Annual Unsupported Retirement Expenses by 20 to calculate your Retirement Fund Target.

Step 17: Develop a detailed Retirement Savings Plan.

Step 18: Adjust your annual savings rate and your retirement spending rate until your Retirement Savings Plan works.

APPENDIX 1

EFC CALCULATION WORKSHEET

Begin with:
Gross Income[1] _____

Subtract:
Federal Income Tax[2] _____
and FICA Tax[2] _____
and State Income Tax[2] _____

= After Tax Income _____

Subtract:
Employment Allowance[3] _____
and Income Protection Allowance[4] _____

= Available Income _____

Begin again with:
Total Assets[5] _____
Subtract:
Asset Protection Allowance[6] _____

= Assessable Assets _____

Multiply by 12%:

= Assessment on Assets _____

Add (from above)
Available Income _____
plus Assessment on Assets _____

= Adjusted Available Income _____

Your EFC is based on your Adjusted Available Income (AAI).
To Calculate your EFC:

AAI < $14,500:	multiply AAI by .22
$14,500 <AAI < $18,200	subtract $14,500 from AAI, multiply the difference by .25, and add $3,124
$18,200 <AAI < $21,900	subtract $18,200 from AAI, multiply the difference by .29, and add $4,024
$21,900 <AAI < $25,600	subtract $21,900 from AAI, multiply the difference by .34, and add $5,068
$25,600 <AAI < $29,300	subtract $25,600 from AAI, multiply the difference by .40, and add $6,292
$29,300 < AAI	subtract $29,300 from AAI, multiply the difference by .47, and add $7,732.

[1] Gross income includes all income from all sources

[2] For all taxes, use the amount from your tax return. For future projections, multiply this number by the same amount as you project your gross income to increase. For example, if your gross income when your child is college age will be 1.3x what it is today, multiply your tax by 1.3.

[3] Use $3,500 if both parents work or $0 if one parent does not work

[4] For the Income Protection Allowance, use the following chart:

# of Family Members (including student)	1 Person in College (including student)	2 People in College (including student)	3 People in College (including student)	4 People in College (including student)	5 People in College (including student)
2	$16,230	$13,450			
3	20,210	17,450	$14,670		
4	24,970	22,190	19,430	$16,650	
5	29,460	26,680	23,920	21,140	$18,380
6	34,460	31,680	28,920	26,140	23,380

For each additional family member above 6, add $3,890. For each additional college student, subtract $2,760.

[5] Do not include money in 401k, IRA, or other designated retirement plans.

[6] For the Asset Protection Allowance, use the following chart. Make sure to use the age the parent will be when the child is a college freshman:

Age of Older Parent in Household	Two Parent Family	One Parent Family
39 or less	$38,700	$15,300
40-44	43,300	17,100
45-49	48,900	19,100
50-54	55,500	21,500
55-59	63,500	24,300
60-64	73,200	27,800
65 or more	80,300	30,100

APPENDIX 2

GROSS INCOME TO NET INCOME
CONVERSION TABLE

Round your projected Gross Income to the nearest number:	Multiply by the number below to calculate your Net Income
$50,000	.72
$60,000	.71
$70,000	.70
$80,000	.70
$90,000	.69
$100,000	.69
$120,000	.68
$140,000	.67
$160,000	.66
$180,000	.66
$200,000	.65
$225,000	.64
$250,000	.64
$275,000	.63
$300,000	.63
$350,000	.62

APPENDIX 3

PERCENT INCREASE IN SOCIAL SECURITY BENEFIT FOR
RETIRING AT AGE 67
(Applies to people born prior to 1960)

Year of Birth	Percent Increase in Social Security Benefit
1924	6%
1925-26	7%
1927-28	8%
1929-30	9%
1931-32	10%
1933-34	11%
1935-36	12%
1937	13%
1938	11.92%
1939	11.67%
1940	10.5%
1941	10%
1942	8.75%
1943-54	8%
1955	6.67%
1956	5.33%
1957	4%
1958	2.67%
1959	1.33%

APPENDIX 4

SOCIAL SECURITY INDEX FACTORS

For Earnings Received in the Year:	Multiply by this Amount to Calculate Average Indexed Earnings
1951	14.43
1952	13.59
1953	12.87
1954	12.80
1955	12.24
1956	11.44
1957	11.10
1958	11.00
1959	10.48
1960	10.08
1961	9.89
1962	9.42
1963	9.19
1964	8.83
1965	8.67
1966	8.18
1967	7.75
1968	7.25
1969	6.86
1970	6.53
1971	6.22
1972	5.66
1973	5.33
1974	5.03
1975	4.68
1976	4.38
1977	4.13
1978	3.83

1979	3.52
1980	3.23
1981	2.93
1982	2.78
1983	2.65
1984	2.50
1985	2.40
1986	2.33
1987	2.19
1988	2.09
1989	2.01
1990	1.92
1991	1.85
1992	1.76
1993	1.75
1994	1.70
1995	1.64
1996	1.56
1997	1.47
1998	1.40
1999	1.33
2000	1.26
2001	1.23
2002	1.22
2003	1.19
2004	1.13
2005	1.09
2006	1.05
2007	1.00
2008	1.00

Visit my website: www.dougwarshauer.com

A book is the ideal vehicle for *teaching*. It is less than ideal for helping people *apply* their knowledge. That is where my website comes in. I have created numerous printable forms and downloadable spreadsheets for you to input your own personal information and easily build your Lifetime Financial Plan. On my website you'll find:

- o **Annual Household Net Income Worksheet**
- o **Annual Household Expenditure Worksheet**
- o **Debt Payoff Worksheet**
- o **Lifetime Auto Purchase Calculator**
- o **Home Purchase Calculator**
- o **Renting vs. Buying Comparison**
- o **Financial Aid Expected Family Contribution Estimator**
- o **Future Earnings Calculator**
- o **College Fund Target Calculator**
- o **College Savings Rate Calculator**
- o **Peak Net Income Calculator**
- o **Expected Retirement Spending Calculator**
- o **Life Expectancy Calculator**
- o **Expected Social Security Benefit Calculator**
- o **Retirement Fund Target Calculator**
- o **Retirement Savings Plan Builder**
  and much more!

Plus, my website is continually updated with in-depth discussions and new information on all the subjects covered in the book, any relevant changes in government regulations and tax policies, and other timely or topical issues.

You can achieve lasting wealth!

Doug Warshauer

Buy Additional Copies of
If I'm So Smart…Where Did All My Money Go?

FREE SHIPPING TO U.S. ADDRESSES

Four easy ways to order:

Fax Orders: 847-470-0581

Phone Orders: 800-262-6355

Email Orders: orders@CFMBbooks.com

Postal Orders: CFMB Books
8264 Lehigh Avenue
Morton Grove, IL 60053

Shipping Information

Name: _____

Street: _____

City, State, Zip: _____

Telephone: _____

Price: $24.95
Please add $2.50 sales tax to orders shipped to Illinois addresses.

Payment Information

__Check   __Visa   __MasterCard   __AMEX   __Discover

Card Number: _____

Name on Card: _____

Expiration Date: _____

For information on bulk purchases of *If I'm So Smart…Where Did All My Money Go?*, please contact CFMB Books at 8264 Lehigh Avenue, Morton Grove, IL 60053. Phone: 800-262-6355.